Those Controversial Gifts

Prophecy Dreams Visions Tongues Interpretation Healing

George Mallone

with contributions from
John Opmeer,
Jeff Kirby and
Paul Stevens

Foreword by Michael Green

InterVarsity Press
Downers Grove
Illinois 60515

InterVarsity Press is the book-publishing division of Inter-Varsity Christian Fellowship, a student movement active on campus at hundreds of universities, colleges and schools of nursing. For information about local and regional activities, write IVCF, 233 Langdon St., Madison, WI 53703.

Distributed in Canada through InterVarsity Press, 860 Denison St., Unit 3, Markham, Ontario L3R 4H1, Canada.

All quotations from the Scripture, unless otherwise noted, are from the Revised Standard Version of the Bible, copyrighted 1946, 1952, © 1971, 1973.

Cover photograph: Robert McKendrick.

ISBN 0-87784-823-8

Printed in the United States of America

Library of Congress Cataloging in Publications Data

Mallone, George, 1944-
     Those controversial gifts.

     Includes bibliographical references and index.
     1.   Gifts, Spiritual–Addresses, essays, lectures.
I.   Title.
BT767.3.M325   1983   234'.13   83-8
ISBN 0-87784-823-8

17	16	15	14	13	12	11	10	9	8	7	6	5	4	3	2	1
95	94	93	92	91	90	89	88	87	86	85	84	83				

*To our brothers and sisters
who faithfully pray with us fortnightly
and encourage us to exercise all the gifts
of the Holy Spirit.*

Foreword

I am delighted to commend this book, and I am confident it will be extremely useful in many churches. I have had the pleasure of knowing George Mallone both before and after the change of understanding he has undergone concerning the gifts of the Holy Spirit. As one who has trod a somewhat similar path in recent years, I welcome this book for a number of reasons.

In the first place it is a courageous book. Nobody can write on a subject as potentially explosive as this without knowing that his readers are likely to be divided in their reactions. The traditionalists in both Reformed and Dispensational camps are unlikely to give it total endorsement, but I hope the careful argument and irenic stance will enable many people to appreciate that you cannot fasten God down in a box of any description. He is the Living God who is always liable to make himself known in ways the dogmatic theologian had not bargained for.

Second, this is a bridge-building book. There is no yawning gap here between charismatics and noncharismatics.

The whole linguistic label is distasteful and misleading, and George Mallone does not use it. He believes that the spiritual gifts of New Testament days have not been withdrawn, but he does not believe there are two types of Christian, nor that a second experience of the Holy Spirit is indispensable, nor that speaking in tongues is the necessary mark of being filled with the Spirit. Often in North America Christians allow themselves to be acutely polarized on this issue. Here is a book which will make for unity, understanding and love.

Third, I salute this book because it is a shared work. If the renewal movement stands for anything, it stands for the recovery of every member ministry under the impulse of the Holy Spirit. No one has all the gifts. Accordingly, it is entirely appropriate that three of the chapters have been written by his Vancouver colleagues. Paul Stevens's contribution on how these spiritual gifts can actually be developed and used in a congregation is particularly valuable.

Finally, I rejoice in this book because it is so practical. It is not another tiresome treatise for or against charismatic gifts—the presses have been groaning with such books for a decade. No, this book is something different. It shows how sane, vital evangelical churches in the Vancouver area have welcomed these spiritual gifts and have greatly enriched their lives. There is nothing extravagant or bizarre here. The authors do not get spiritual gifts out of proportion. They show how the generous equipment the Spirit gives to members of Christ's body can be discovered and encouraged. There is a delightful mixture on these pages of doctrine and experience, of encouragement and warning, of sanity and faith. There are few churches, whatever their experience of spiritual gifts, who would not find fresh insights and wise counsel in this book. I am confident it will do much good.

Michael Green

Preface

None of the writers of this volume considers himself, in the popular sense of the word, a "charismatic pastor of a charismatic church." First and foremost we view ourselves as evangelicals who believe in the fullness of the Holy Spirit and the exercise of all the gifts of the Holy Spirit. Our backgrounds, both Dispensational and Reformed, taught us to believe that the overt gifts of the Holy Spirit ceased with the apostles. To pass our theological exams we all adopted the party line. After varying lengths of time in pastoral ministry, however, each of us came to the same basic conclusions: (1) the cessation of particular gifts was not taught in Scripture; (2) the church was desperately weak and anemic because of the lack of these gifts; and (3) what we were seeing in our own experience suggested that these gifts were available for the church today.

No doubt some evangelicals will think this book goes too far. Some pentecostals will think it does not go far enough. For those who are presently unsure about spiritual gifts, we hope it will be an exhortation to faith in a living God who does wondrous things even in our own day. We also hope to encourage others who believe the gifts of the Spirit have not ceased to come out of the closet and to begin to proclaim and practice these gifts in local churches.

Chapter one tackles the question of the supposed cessation of these gifts. Then follow chapters on prophecy (two), dreams and visions (three), tongues and interpretation (four), and healing (five). Chapter six shifts to practical principles for training people in the use of their gifts. The last chapter confronts the issue of fear and how it inhibits the manifestation of these gifts. The appendix is a valuable statement produced by a group of British church leaders on the work of the Spirit.

Our prayer is that the church of Jesus Christ might be renewed. We have no preconceived notion of what that must look like, only the settled conviction that it is needed. Reviving the gifts of the Holy Spirit is only one small part of the total picture. Only when each part has been placed into the life of the church will there be the assurance that "his Bride has made herself ready" (Rev 19:7) and is now awaiting the great marriage supper of the Lamb.

Our thanks to Charles Hummel, Howard Snyder, Calvin Chambers and Nancy Nichols, who gave suggestions and criticism, and to Marion Gorrie and Mary-Margaret Cote, who typed the manuscript.

1
Tidy Doctrine and Truncated Experience
George Mallone

"A year ago in a moment of either cynicism or realism, I said to Arnold Bittlinger about the charismatic renewal, 'It is two-thirds phony,' and he replied, 'Yes, but one-third is a lot.' "[1]

This frank admission by Thomas A. Smail, editor of *Theological Renewal* and one of the foremost thinkers in the charismatic movement in Great Britain, will no doubt elicit a hearty amen from many. It seems that for some time some charismatic leaders have played a game of "who's fooling who" with those of us who are skeptical of their claims of revelations and healings. Any thoughtful observer of the movement has easily discerned the spiritual hyperbole and outlandish tomfoolery that has gone on in the name of the Holy Spirit. Yet, as Bittlinger has pointed out, one-third is a lot.

The suggestion that two-thirds of the charismatic movement is false is no doubt overstatement. There are many inadequacies to be sure, and God alone knows the percentage. Yet a portion of the renewal is from God, and it is this genuine one-third of gift renewal that is our present concern. It is possible for all the gifts of the Holy Spirit to function in the church today. For this to be a reality, however, it is necessary for us to clear a series of theological and exegetical roadblocks which have been placed in our way since the death of the apostles. As in the repair of an old road, some blasting is often necessary before repaving.

Arguments for Cessation

For hundreds of years, theologians and churchmen have circulated arguments to prove that certain gifts of the Holy Spirit ceased with the apostles. My own dispensationalism specialized in one of these arguments—a question of exegesis of 1 Corinthians 13. I shall never forget my first venture to a graduate library to find out what other exegetes had to say about this verse. I searched commentary after commentary, but none supported the position of my tradition. If it was such a defensible argument, why did other evangelicals not recognize it? With not one supporter to be found, I sat down to review my traditional catechism.

Although I was not sure about it, I began to smell a skunk in the woodshed. Could it be that these sincere believers had formulated for themselves a theology of reaction? Had they seen something which they did not appreciate and then gone to Scripture to prove that it did not exist? These and many other questions plagued me for that year. Finally, I learned a helpful principle: the simplest explanation for a verse of Scripture is usually the best, and obscure passages of Scripture must always give way to clear passages.[2] Thus, although I had not settled my theological or experiential convictions about the matter, "Do not forbid speaking in tongues" (1 Cor 14:39) became my basis for understanding the somewhat more complicated set of verses "For tongues, they will cease . . . when the perfect comes" (1 Cor 13:8-10).

I have learned much from those who have argued for

the ceasing of certain gifts. I must say, however, that I have not found their arguments to be compelling. There have been times when I wished they were valid, for they would have saved me much pastoral disturbance and inward restlessness. As fairly as I possibly can, then, I will summarize the main arguments for cessation (exegetical, theological, historical and experiential) before presenting a refutation.

Exegesis. There are three Scripture verses which have been used to defend this position. Some say that 1 Corinthians 13:8-10 suggests that certain gifts ceased with the complete formation of the canon, the "perfect" of verse 10 being Scripture.[3] Revelation 22:18 is used to refute any present-day exercise of the gift of prophecy. According to this interpretation, prophecy is seen as adding to God's already completed revelation.[4] Ephesians 2:20 is used to suggest that the apostles, those who were eyewitnesses to Christ's resurrection and inspired to write Holy Scripture, laid the foundation for the church and hence this gift is no longer needed.

Theology. Many modern theologians would deny the presence of such gifts today because they assume that they were not present in the first century. The biblical record of such events is just part and parcel of the mythology that grew up around "the Christ event." By contrast, evangelical theologians, while affirming the reality of these gifts within the first century, have nevertheless used various arguments to show cessation. One school of thought, dispensationalism, suggests that in various periods of history God works in unique ways to perform his purpose.[5] Thus, for example, the use of miracles in Jesus' mission to Israel and in the launching of the church pictured in Acts is specific to that dispensation or period. But miracles are not appropriate in this present dispensation.

Covenant theologians, most notably B. B. Warfield, suggest that certain gifts were clustered in association with periods of God's revelation.[6] The exodus from Egypt and the giving of the Law at Sinai marked the time of one cluster; the time of Elijah and Elisha marked another; the ministry of Jesus and the apostles marked the final cluster. In each period, so-called miraculous gifts were meant to give divine authenticity to new revelation. But since the revelation is now complete through God's Son and God's Word, these gifts are no longer necessary.

Another strong theological argument stems from the withdrawing of the apostolic office. The leaders of the Protestant Reformation constantly pointed out that apostolic succession lacked any biblical support. Thus, they concluded that if one of the major gifts of the Spirit (that of being an apostle) had ceased in its operation, or was only temporary, then it was possible and indeed probable that others were also temporary.

History. It is claimed that some gifts, most notably tongues, prophecy and healing, with only a few exceptions, did not exist in the church after the apostolic period. Any manifestations of this kind after the time of the apostles were supposedly confined to emotional and heretical movements such as the Montanists, the followers of Edward Irving and the Shakers of Mother Ann Lee.[7]

Experience. "Having had about a dozen persons in the congregation who speak in tongues, I have had to come to some hard conclusions after a year of effort. . . . It was obvious that they had a spiritual superiority complex. . . . These persons are insensitive to the concept of Christian discipline . . . they are unteachable . . . tend to split churches . . . become church hoppers. . . . I am convinced that they do not have the Holy Spirit. They were possessed with a counterfeit, a fake, they were living on an ego trip, a manufactured religious high."[8]

This common concern has been echoed in church after church in North America. As in this case, people have genuinely reached out and embraced those who claimed particular gifts. But it did not take long before the whole thing erupted into chaos. Others, less charitable, have labeled any renewal of the gifts to be a "satanic counterfeit," while still others suggest the behavior is emotionally unstable.[9]

Arguments against Cessation

Abuses in the name of the Holy Spirit are today legion. Cooking with "miracle whip" is expected to give one a new religious experience, and exorcising a "devil's food cake" becomes a test of your spirituality. But we should not let these zany claims obscure the testimony of God's longing to speak to his people and to heal them of their infirmities. If there are valid exegetical and theological arguments for cessation, then let us go no further. Yet if these arguments are invalid, then we must proceed to apprehend that which God has fully and freely given.

Exegesis. Nowhere in Scripture does it state that the gifts of the Spirit have ceased. Arguments which suggest that Scripture supports this position are usually bad exegesis, a deduction from theology or an argument from the silence of Scripture. The "perfect" of 1 Corinthians 13:10, for example, cannot be taken to mean canonized Scripture. Paul is contrasting the partial with the complete, things that befit a child versus things that commend adulthood. The focal point for advance is the appearance of the "perfect." The Greek word *teleios* simply means "end," "purpose" or "completion."[10] Inherent in the word is no concept of a written record. This is simply a theological deduction. We are left to observe the text to see if it helps us to define the word by its use in its context.

Fortunately, verse 12 uses two images that help us perceive the coming of the "perfect." Paul's present state was to be compared to seeing one's face in a polished metal mirror. Although you could make out the image, it still was unclear. Paul, having had the words of Jesus personally given to him (Gal 1:12), could speak of a partial knowledge. Even those who maintain the highest respect for Scripture today confess that while it tells us everything we *need* to know, it does not give us all we *might know* or *would like* to know. The second image suggests that with the "perfect" comes a full face-to-face encounter with Jesus Christ—at his Second Coming. We shall see him just as he is (1 Jn 3:2). At that moment, all human knowledge will pass away and shall be replaced by heavenly knowledge granted the children of God. Until that moment arrives all that is contained in God's Word and given to us by his Holy Spirit will be necessary for the church's life. There is no justification from this text to pronounce a cessation of certain gifts.

With a faulty conclusion from 1 Corinthians 13:10 as a foundation, it is further deduced from Revelation 22:18-19 that prophecy ceased to exist with the closure of the canon. However, John's prohibition is not to all prophecy, but to the deliberate falsification of the one given to him by the Holy Spirit. That Revelation is the last book in our New Testament canon does not mean it was the last to be written or the final canonical prophecy given.

A more serious argument than either of these two can be presented from Ephesians 2:20. If the foundation of the church has been laid by the apostles and prophets, then there is no reason for these functions to continue. With this same reasoning, the Reformers debunked apostolic succession on the conviction that there was no scriptural support for the idea (Mt 16:18). Again, however, this is a theological deduction from the text and not something which the text explicitly states. The intention of this verse is not to say that these gifts have ceased but only that any gift exercised must be in harmony with the instructions of the founding apostles and prophets. As John Stott says, "In practical terms this means that the church is built on the New Testament documents."[11] In chapter two we will show how this harmony is discerned and protected.

Other flaws in the cessationist fabric are the narrow definitions given to prophecy and apostleship. According to some, prophecy can only refer to giving new revelation and an apostle can only be one who was an eyewitness of Christ's resurrection. Although essentially correct, these definitions are too restrictive. The word *prophecy* can be used for revelation or for an explanation of the revelation already given. Zechariah, when filled with the Holy Spirit, prophesied (Lk 1:67-79). The content of his word is not new revelation but an announcement that the Old Testament revelation had been fulfilled and was now to be his and Israel's experience. It was prophecy for edification, exhortation and consolation (1 Cor 14:3). Likewise, apostles were not only those who saw the resurrected Lord, but also those who had been gifted by the Lord for planting churches and advancing the gospel (Acts 14:14; Rom 16:7).

In summary, to state that some gifts have ceased and others have not is to go further than Scripture allows. Scripture teaches us how to regulate and exercise these gifts and how to test their validity. But only when Jesus Christ comes again are we to expect their cessation.

Theology. When I made my first application to seminary, a friend gave me this questionable advice: "You can't choose the right seminary until you know what theology you believe." I gave a rather intelligent "huh" to his remark and then responded by saying, "I thought you went to seminary to find out what the Bible said in order to formulate your theology?" "Not so!" said my friend, and he showed me some seminary catalogs which insisted that applicants sign an extensive theological statement. That experience highlights the controversy we are about to look at now: Should we believe theological deductions which have little or no explicit scriptural support?

Through dispensational glasses we are taught to see separate economies in which God works in successive and unique ways with his people. For this reason some gifts, assigned to one economy and not to another, are then considered to be temporary while others are permanent. We are told to see the Spirit's activity through certain gifts in the early church but not to expect it now, and that it will recommence during a literal seven-year tribulation (Rev 11:1-13). This cutting up of Scripture contradicts a basic rule of hermeneutics, namely, the simplicity and transparency of Scripture (the perspicuity of Scripture). It introduces the view that part of the New Testament text is not directed to postapostolic Christians and in that sense it is therefore not God's Word for today. But surely Scripture is not to be divided like this. Not only would this make God a God of confusion, but it would be impossible for the unschooled to read Scripture at face value. Scripture mixes and mingles the gifts of the Spirit without ever attempting to place them in some stratified catalog of temporary or permanent, miraculous or nonmiraculous.

B. B. Warfield's teaching on cessation of the gifts has now influenced almost an entire century of the church's life. Picking up from the Reformers, Warfield maintained that certain gifts were given to accredit God's heaven-sent revelation. The exodus, Sinai, Elijah and Elisha, Jesus and the apostles were the only persons and events around which God revealed himself in such a fashion.

To be valid, such a theory needs to pass the scrutiny of some hard questions. First, why are Elijah and Elisha included in this category? Theirs was no new period of biblical revelation (1 Kings 16—19). Granted, Israel was in precaptivity apostasy and in need of God's renewing touch, but compared with the giving of the law, the teachings of Jesus and the new age of the Spirit, what *new* revelation was given in this period? Besides, most of the miracles were done in private, out of the view of the nation (1 Kings 17:22-23; 2 Kings 2:11-14, 19-22; 4:32-37; 5:14; 6:5-7; 13:21). Surely these two persons have simply been shoved into this category so that all miraculous events can be fit into a tidy category.

Second, were these miracles done only as attesting signs of God's revelation? As we will show in chapter five, the healing ministry of the church is commanded as an ongoing obligation (Jas 5:15-18). James goes on to explain that this type of ministry models the work of Elijah. Jesus' ministry of healing the sick and preaching the good news sprang out of a deep compassion for those who had no shepherd (Mt 9:36), not as a technique for convincing men of his deity.

Third, if these gifts were given to authenticate the apostolic message, why did some who were not apostles exercise these gifts (Acts 8:6; 14:3) and why were these gifts given to the congregation at Corinth in which no apostle lived?[12]

Recently John MacArthur, in an effort to safeguard a closed canon, accused all noncessationists of neo-orthodoxy.[13] His assumption is that those who believe the gifts continue must be discontent with Scripture because they want to add new revelation to it with their prophecies and other gifts. To my knowledge no noncessationist in the mainstream of Christianity claims that revelation today is equal with Scripture. The lunatic fringe and cults will possibly say so, but no evangelical will make this claim. As we will show in chapter two, prophecy today does not pretend to be a normative teaching for the church, but is understood to be for "upbuilding and encouragement and consolation" (1 Cor 14:3). Far from adding to God's Word, today's prophecies will invariably summon God's people back to observance of the new covenant, just as the Old Testament prophets called the Israelites back to the old covenant. To claim that all noncessationists are neo-orthodox is unfounded sensationalism and only heightens the conviction uttered by Tertullian that it was the bishops who expelled prophecy and not the canon of Scripture.

Another area of confusion is the assumption that all non-cessationists reason from pentecostal hermeneutics. It is assumed that all subscribe to the classic pentecostal framework of the baptism of the Holy Spirit as a second work of grace, evidenced by speaking in tongues. But this is not true. Many evangelicals openly teach and practice all the gifts of the Spirit without adopting pentecostal theology. That we reject pentecostal theology, however, does not mean we are forced to conclude that the gifts are not for today. The gifts belong to the church and will continue to belong to the church until the end of the age. Their benefit and enjoyment does not depend on any particular theological point of view, and we should not let theological extrapolations rob us of the gifts that God wants to give.

History. All observers of postapostolic history are aware of the decline of certain gifts in the church. Decline, however, is vastly different from withdrawal. Those who argue that certain gifts have ceased often fail to acknowledge their working assumption, namely, that silence on the subject denotes absence. Nor is it appropriate to argue just the opposite, that silence means the presence of these activities.

We are on the safest ground when we realize the following points suggested by Harold Hunter.[14] First, the post-apostolic fathers wrote about certain phenomena either because of the abuse of these phenomena or their academic interest in them. Second, many records were not kept because of the expected imminent return of Christ. Third, many of the most valuable records on this subject were lost or destroyed. Fourth, the fact that none of the church fathers set out to write a complete systematic theology or elaborate commentary on the New Testament has left us somewhat short-handed. Fifth, modern historical research is often hampered in objective analysis due to certain theological blinders which demand a predetermined result.

There is sufficient evidence to suggest that controversial gifts did continue after the apostles, in spite of obscurities in some of the writings of the postapostolic Fathers. Michael Green suggests that Ignatius (ca 35-ca 107) was personally used to give words of prophecy.[15] The churches of Lyons and Vienne wrote to the churches of Asia and Phrygia about persecution and mentioned a Phrygian physician named Alexander who was "not without a share of the apostolic grace [charisma]."[16] Papias (ca 60-130), bishop of Hierapolis in Phrygia, claimed to have been told by the daughters of Philip of the resuscitation of a man from the dead.[17] Justin Martyr (100-165), said to be a friend of cessationists, claimed that "it is possible now to see among us men and women who possess gifts of the Spirit of God."[18] Irenaeus (130-200) spoke of prophecies, healings and tongues which were uttered in his day.[19] Hippolytus (ca 170-ca 236), presbyter and teacher in Rome, wrote a work entitled "On Charismatic Gifts" which has been lost. In his writings that are available, he wrote, "If anyone says, 'I have received the gift of healing,' hands shall not be laid upon him: the deed shall make manifest if he speaks the truth."[20] Tertullian (160-215) wrote a seven-volume work entitled *Ecstasy* that also has been lost. Tertullian has much to say about the charismata even in his pre-Montanist writing. He later relates a story of a woman who often had visions during the church service and waited until the conclusion of the worship to pass on her experience. Tertullian introduces the account with these words: "For, seeing that we acknowledge spiritual *charismata,* or gifts, we too have merited the attainment of the prophetic gift."[21] In later accounts he defends and encourages speaking in tongues.[22] Cyril of Jerusalem (310-386) thought it was not impossible for baptismal candidates to prophesy once they came out of the water.[23] Origen (185-254) witnessed to gifts such as exorcism, healing and predictions.[24]

Along with this evidence two things must be admitted. First, various fathers, such as Chrysostom, Theodore and Augustine, at certain times denied the reality of these gifts. Augustine in his *Retractions* apologized for his statements and said that he never intended to say that miracles ceased with the apostles:

> But what I said is not to be interpreted that no miracles are believed to be performed in the name of Christ in the present time. For when I wrote that book, I myself had recently learned that a blind man had been restored to sight . . . and I know about some others, so numerous even in these times, that we cannot know about all of them or enumerate those we know.[25]

Second, many movements which possessed these gifts, such as the second-century Montanists, threatened the institutional church and bordered on heresy in some of their doctrine. They were movements of reaction, and "they overdid what other Christians underdid."[26]

Although sufficient evidence abounds to show that particular gifts did exist after the time of the apostles, a bigger question needs to be raised: Why have these gifts declined in breadth and power from the first century until today? First, with the rise of clericalism within the church, these outstanding gifts were given to the officeholders of apostolic succession. "That led inevitably to institutional ecclesiasticism, and the inevitable corresponding loss of the church's awareness of the Spirit's presence and experience of the Spirit's power."[27] As John Wesley said in 1750, "The grand reason why the miraculous gifts were so soon withdrawn was not only that faith and holiness were well nigh lost, but that dry, formal, orthodox men began then to ridicule whatever gifts they had not themselves and to cry them all as evil madness or imposture."[28] There was also a strong reaction by church leaders to the ignorance and credulity of the laity in matters relating to miracles. Magic and mysticism were easily confused with the true working of God. Therefore it was necessary for bishops to confirm all spiritual activities in order to maintain purity. This in itself, while it assumed a good purpose, froze out much of the genuine work of God. As the church moved to greater institutionalism during the reign of Constantine, it only furthered the institutional performance expected of the Holy Spirit.

Second, history seems to witness the pridefulness of human intellect in and through the rise of scientism, which confessed itself sufficient without God. This stepchild of modern humanism denied God's presence in human affairs and his ability to intervene at any moment.

Third, John Calvin says that these gifts were lost out of ingratitude.[29] A church which had lost its heart for the Lord had become more pagan than Christian and had turned its back on that which God called a gift to the church. John Wesley observed a similar correlation between the loss of gifts and the general state of the church: "The causes of their decline was not as has been vulgarly supposed because there is no more need for them, because all the world were become Christians. . . . The real cause was: the love of many, almost all Christians so-called, was waxed cold . . . this was the real cause why the extraordinary gifts of the Holy Spirit were no longer to be found in the Christian church: because the Christians were turned heathen again and had only a dead form left."[30] Orthodoxy remained, but with diminished expectations. Unbelief reigned. The church had accommodated itself to secularism and thus lost all its power.

Experience. There is no doubt that the vigor of renewal and the accompanying gifts of the Holy Spirit do bring a creative stir to the church. But it need not be a divisive experience. Most of the authors of this book pastor evangelical churches which believe in and exercise all the gifts of the Spirit. Not all the members have the same gifts, yet there is no feeling of first-class or second-class citizenship and no major hassle connected with the exercise of these gifts.

Divisions, when they do appear, rise out of carnality on the part of both those who have and have not received certain spiritual gifts. Absolute dogmatism regarding the withdrawal of a gift which a brother or sister claims to possess makes that person defensive. Likewise, any manifestation of pride or spiritual superiority on the part of those who have received certain gifts may often offend those who have not. In both cases carnality is at work. Scripture maintains that we are not to despise the gift of prophecy (1 Thess 5:20) nor forbid the speaking of tongues (1 Cor 14:39). Likewise we are not to judge the spiritual temperature of a brother or sister or to despise them for not having certain gifts (1 Cor 12:29-30). In love we are to receive one another and forgive the blunders we make with each other in receiving these gifts back to the church.

I remember vividly how God introduced these gifts into our own fellowship. Arriving back from a summer holiday, I noticed that a charismatic fever had been caught by some of our members. My immediate reaction was to stamp it out as quickly as possible before it spread. I began to notice in the lives of certain people, however, a genuine spiritual renewal. My next step was to attempt to teach rather than to stamp out. But as I began to teach I found that I, as a cessationist, had much to learn also. About that time, God sent us a couple from England who had the experience of living in harmony with those who manifested particular gifts as well as those who did not. Not so much through their teaching as through their modeling of love and gentle acceptance, we began to grow in love toward one another. It was this love which was able to cast out all fear regarding the re-entrance of these particular gifts. It was love and loyalty toward one another that freely allowed the gifts to function.

Welcome Spiritual Gifts

As spiritual gifts begin to re-emerge in the church, there are several things we must be aware of. First, Satan wants to divide the church. He will take any opportunity to breach the wall. Yet this should not cause us to retreat into the security of uniformity, thinking that as long as we all do the same thing then Satan cannot get to us. But in that case we would simply be asleep and no threat to him. This approach is only an attempt to be united at the lowest levels. What the church needs in order to stand strong is unity in diversity, not unity in conformity. Only when all the gifts function in harmony, toward building one another up, will we be able to stand strong against the opposing winds (Eph 4:11-16).

Second, the authentic sign of the Holy Spirit's presence is fruit (Gal 5), character (Mt 5), and submission (Eph 5:18-21), not gifts. If a person claims to have a particular gift, yet does not manifest the fruit of the Spirit, his gift is not necessarily invalid. Likewise, one who claims the gifts are withdrawn may also lack the fruit of the Holy Spirit. Lacking fruit does not invalidate the claims of either but only points out the need for spiritual maturity. In a climate of mature Christianity, the fruit of the Spirit will allow acceptance, gentleness and even different convictions to be held together in the bond of love. To expel members with whom we do not agree shows not our orthodoxy but our lack of maturity.

Third, much of the knee-jerk reaction to particular gifts comes out of relational fears and prejudices. Our likes and dislikes get in the way of Christ's lordship. In a community which is lubricated with love, however, one brother or sister may often lead another out of the bondage of fear of the gifts to show them that they are not as esoteric or as weird as they have been made out to be. They are simply expressions of our genuine humanity under the control and use of the Holy Spirit. Loving exposure is the best teacher to those who are fearful. I am so thankful to the men and women who have modeled this type of maturity in my period of skepticism over the genuineness of the gifts. Again, perfect love will cast out the fear (1 Jn 4:18).

Finally, in a way known only to God, every person is challenged to a new level of commitment to Christ's lordship when all the gifts are returned to the church. It is no longer possible to live with comfortable cerebralism or tidy doctrine. The Holy Spirit will come and begin to point out any truncation in our experience. No doubt this will be threatening at first. But let each of us remember that Christ's call to discipleship is personal, meaning that it comes to each of us in our own time and in our own unique way. Therefore, being pushy with one another is completely off limits. It is incumbent on each Christian to be open to the greater working of God in his or her life and to exercise what God has given each of us within the body.

A New Reformation?
The Reformers did the church a great service in retrieving some doctrines from Scripture which had been lost for many centuries. By grace alone, by faith alone, by Scripture alone, is now our meat and drink. If it is true that such crucial doctrines were lost yet brought back to the church, can it not be possible within the twentieth century that God desires the church to rediscover the doctrine and practice of all the gifts of the Holy Spirit, many of which have been neglected or feared for some 1800 years? Could this be the beginning of a new reformation for the church? Is it not time for the church to practice the priesthood of

believers and to acknowledge that their equipment for ministry is more than serving tea, counting money or folding chairs? I believe it is.

The devil, our ancient foe, has not ceased his struggle to subdue the light of God. Even at this last hour he is desperately trying to win the pre-eminence he lost at the cross. To defeat his works and to be the prepared bride of Christ the church needs all the gifts and armament God has provided. To despise these gifts, either by theological negation or practical skepticism, will leave us wholly unequipped to meet the battle.

2
Thus Says the Lord: Prophecy and Discernment
George Mallone

In December 1973 I was scheduled to speak to a group of Christian professional women at an evangelistic dinner party. The day before the dinner I developed a severe case of laryngitis. After drafting a close friend to bail me out if worse came to worst, I choked down a quart of "Granny Greensprings" and spent the afternoon before the party sleeping. While I was asleep a very distinct picture came to my mind: I dreamed that I was surrounded in a white jacket much like those used to restrain psychiatric patients. Awaking from my sleep, I thought I was uncomfortable because of my bulky sweater; so I took it off and went back to sleep. A second time I had the same vivid picture in my mind. I awoke again, this time removing the comforter from my bed. A third time this very vivid picture came to mind while I slept, but when I awoke this time the Lord clearly gave me the interpretation for the picture which I had been seeing. He said to me, "You are surrounded in my love, and you are surrounded in my grace." The word was so profound I fell back on the bed in amazement. Sensing that God was speaking and giving direction for the evening,

I dressed and went to the dinner party. While driving into the city, I spoke to the Lord about the dream. Unsure whether the dream was just for me or for someone else, I told him that I was prepared to share it with anyone who could be helped by it.

There were over five hundred women present when I arrived. We went through the formalities of eating and the Christmas program. At last it came my turn to speak. I strapped a microphone close to my mouth and began. But just a few minutes into the presentation the Lord seemed to lay upon me the necessity of sharing what had happened that afternoon. As I came to the word, "You are surrounded in my love and in my grace," the Lord powerfully converted a woman, a Jehovah's Witness, sitting only three rows from me. As with Lydia (Acts 16:14), God opened her heart and filled her with his grace. Crying later that evening, she told me that it was not just the gospel message that softened her heart, but the intimate communication that God gave to her through the dream. It had opened her eyes to receive all Christ had done for her at Calvary. Through a gift of prophecy, this time through a dream, God spoke his dynamic word to this new sister.

Paul wrote to the leaders at Thessalonica admonishing them to stop rejecting prophetic activity (1 Thess 5:20-22). If there is no biblical reason for suggesting that the gift of prophecy has ceased, then the Thessalonian admonishment is to be heeded by the church today. In balance it must also be said that if prophecy is to be exercised in the church, then it must be done in a biblical manner. Therefore we need to survey the biblical injunctions and the practical mechanics for the use of this gift and the avoidance of its abuse.

Old Testament Prophets and Prophecy

The hallmark of prophetic activity is that the prophet is

used as a channel for the work of Yahweh.[1] Although Abraham was the first to be called a prophet (Gen 20:7; Ps 105:15), the real genesis of prophetic activity was with Moses. For nearly forty years Moses was under the tutelage of Pharaoh, learning all the linguistic and managerial skills of Egypt. For a second forty years he labored as a shepherd, father and husband. At eighty years (Ex 7:7), Moses was called by Yahweh to be his mouthpiece to both Israel and Egypt.

As with all genuine prophets, the initiative for Moses' call rested with God. Moses did not seek it for himself. In fact he did everything possible to avoid the uncomfortable position of speaking for God (Ex 4:10-17). This reaction gives us our first clue for spotting a person truly called by God to prophetic activity. We should expect to see reluctance in the person rather than presumption. If the person is striving to grasp a prophetic role, demanding to hear a word from the Lord and to give it, then we may question the genuineness of this communication. Humility and reluctance will characterize the prophet. Although the New Testament suggests that there is a place for earnest desire for the gift of prophecy (1 Cor 14:1), the intention is that love should be the controlling motive for the use of the gift (1 Cor 13).

The classical definition of a prophet, one who foretells and forthtells, is an apt description of Moses. He was called to proclaim the predicted release of God's enslaved people (Ex 3:15-22) and to announce the moral imperatives (ethical, religious and social) of following a holy God (Ex 19:1-6).

During Moses' life and before, prophetic activity was localized in one person. But as Moses predicted (Deut 18:18), God was soon to raise up other prophets who would continue this revelatory ministry. Beginning with Samuel (1 Sam 3; 7:5; 8:10), prophetic activity flourished. This

Spirit-inspired activity often led to ecstasy (19:24) which was the fertile soil for prophetic utterances.

Modes of Revelation

With Moses, the mode of revelation was through a theophany, a visible manifestation of Yahweh in the burning bush (Ex 3:4). Discerning how the word of God came to the other prophets, however, is not as simple. We are only told that "the word of the Lord came" (Is 1:1; Joel 1:1; Jon 1:1) and not exactly *how* that word was perceived. In some way the word was so actively present that one could not help but be aware of it. "Inspiration is a miracle: we do not know in what way God makes the mind of man aware of his word."[2]

Dreams and visions played an important part in the revelation to the prophet. While self-induced visions or "dreams of one's own fancy" were called illegitimate (Jer 23:16-40), Scripture commends the use of dreams for revelation (Num 12:6-7; 1 Sam 28:6, 15). Visions or word pictures, such as those given to the prophet Zechariah, were also valid modes of perceiving God's purpose and plan. In some ways Christians have often had their heads in the sand when reading the psychic testimonies of the Old Testament prophets. To some this smacks of Edgar Cayce or Jeanne Dixon and other occultists. The Old Testament assures us, however, that the Holy Spirit is the one who inspired the telepathic and clairvoyant gifts of God's genuine prophets (Num 11:29; 1 Sam 10:6, 10; 19: 20-23; 1 Kings 22:24; Joel 2:28-29; Hos 9:7; Neh 9:30; Mic 3:8; Zech 7:12; see especially 1 Kings 13:2; 2 Kings 6:12; Is 44:28; Ezek 8—11).

Communicating Revelation

Although God did not use sculptors and painters to communicate his word, he did use visual aids in addition to words. And there was variation in the way each prophet

[handwritten margin note: True Prophets need to "stand in the council of the Lord," be sent or appointed by the Lord.]

spoke. Some introduced their written prose or poetry with the formula "thus says the LORD." Others chose to speak in parables (Is 5:1-7) or allegories (2 Sam 12:1-17; Ezek 16; 23), while others dramatized the completeness of God's word. Isaiah walked about naked and barefoot (Is 20:1-3). Ezekiel destroyed a model city and did not mourn the death of his wife (Ezek 4:1-3; 24:15-18). Jeremiah smashed a potter's vessel (Jer 19:10), and Ahijah tore his new coat (1 Kings 11:29).

True and False Prophets
Although the New Testament seems to suggest that ecstatic frenzy is a sign of false or polluted prophecy (1 Cor 14:32), no such disqualification was present within the Old Testament. Nor was there any reason to dispute the prophet's legitimacy simply on the grounds that he was remunerated for his activity. Still, the Old Testament gives three specific ground rules for spotting a false prophet.

First, if a prophet invites you to go off and worship another god, whether creature or spirit, that person is a false prophet and is to be put to death (Deut 13:1-5). Second, if the prophet speaks a word, claiming it to be from the Lord, but later it is discovered that the word had its origin in something other than God, that prophet is to die (Deut 18:20). Last, the false prophet will be spotted if what he speaks does not come true (Deut 18:22), for what God says will always be fulfilled.

Prophecy and Prophets in the New Testament
Jeremiah forecast a day of a new covenant (Jer 31:31-34), under which it would no longer be necessary for one person to tell another about the Lord, for all believers would know the Lord personally. No longer would it be a few chosen individuals who knew the mind and heart of God, for God would put his law into every believer's heart "from the least

Is the act of prophecy then less dramatic now, coming from the law in the believer's heart (God's word internalized) rather than a special revelation?

35

to the greatest." At the coming of the new covenant the petition of Moses became a reality: "Would that all the LORD's people were prophets, that the LORD would put his spirit upon them!" (Num 11:29).

The outpoured Spirit on the day of Pentecost made the prophetic potential of every believer a reality (Acts 2:17-18). Men and women, young and old, each had the potential for the gift of prophecy. "Prophecy" says Gerhard Friedrich, "is not restricted to a few men and women in primitive Christianity. . . . It is a specific mark of the age of fulfillment that the Spirit does not only lay hold of individuals, but that all members of the eschatological community without distinction are called to prophecy."[3]

The prophetic ministry of every believer was undergirded by the words of Jesus. To the disciple it is granted to know the mysteries of the kingdom (Mt 13:11). Jesus refuses now to treat us as slaves but greets us as intimate friends with whom he can share the secrets which his Father has spoken to him (Jn 15:15). And as the prophets of the Old Testament suffered, now we, as prophets of the new covenant, will also suffer (Mt 5:12).[4]

Since Jesus gave himself so completely to us through the Spirit, Paul had no hesitation in encouraging the Corinthians to "earnestly exert" themselves to prophetic ministry (1 Cor 14:1).[5] In fact, they are all allowed to prophesy as long as they do so in accordance with the orderly procedure the apostle lays out (1 Cor 14:26-33). Although not all are gifted as prophets (1 Cor 12:29), each has an enablement by the Spirit to speak God's word.

At the same time, it is also true that the New Testament church recognized specific men and women to be prophets. These individuals were usually itinerant and ministered alongside residential teachers and pastors (Acts 13:1-3). Some, such as Agabus, were noted for their forecasting ability (Acts 11:27-30; 21:10-14). Others like Judas and

Silas, and no doubt the daughters of Philip, "encouraged and strengthened" the churches with lengthy messages (Acts 15:32; 21:9). There were also residential prophets among the elders akin to those at Lystra who laid hands on Timothy and spoke God's appropriate word (1 Tim 1:18; 4:14).

The New Testament balance that all can prophesy, yet some are called to be prophets, needs to be kept in view today. The mantle of prophecy on one person does not preclude other believers from exercising a gift of prophecy. In fact, it is the free access of *all* to prophesy which confirms the ability of any particular prophet.

The modes of revelation of New Testament prophecies were very similar to those in the Old Testament. The Spirit pressed a work or picture upon an individual until personal awareness of that word was received. No doubt there were dreams and visions which preceded some of these words (Mt 1:20; 2:12; Acts 2:17; 9:10-11; 10:3-4; 12:9-10; 16:9-10; 26:19; 2 Cor 12:1; Rev 9:17).

Communicating New Testament Prophecy

The normative context for exercising the gift of prophecy is within the worship service of the church (1 Cor 14:26-27). Aided by both the forms of worship (for example, creedal hymns, vocal amens, the Lord's Prayer, the Eucharist) and its freedoms (each one bringing his or her own Spirit-directed creation), the gift of prophecy flows. It is not seen as a unique gift apart from the others, but one gift flowing with the others in the orchestration of the Spirit.

Some pentecostal conditioning has taught us to believe that the gift of prophecy must be uttered in first-person singular, Elizabethan English. If we can be assured of anything, it is that the primitive church did not use such language. Given that prophecy was tested within the meeting itself (1 Cor 14:29), there probably was a greater sense of humility than we might think pervading prophecy in the early church. It is easy to say "thus says the Lord" when there are not spiritual people around to judge the word. But when such individuals are present, the environment for receiving prophecy changes. Humility and integrity are demanded with any word coming from the Lord.

How was the word delivered? Although we can only speculate, it is not unreasonable, because of the Spirit's creativity, that such words came in written prose or poetry, in spoken or written prayers, in the sharing of a dream or vision, in drama or even dance, in spontaneous singing or in the arrangement of a new hymn. As such words from God were delivered, believers were given substance to their faith (edification), motivation to their faith (exhortation) and comfort in their faith (consolation) (1 Cor 4:3). As the hearts of unbelievers were exposed before God, they were convicted. Falling down on their faces, they confessed that God was surely among these believers (1 Cor 14:25).

Preaching and Prophecy
It is often asked whether the prophet of today is the expository Bible preacher. There certainly is a prophetic character to biblical exposition. The reference to the prophetic ministry of Judas and Silas (Acts 15:32) indicates that prophecy was more than just one or two sentences inspired by the Holy Spirit, and the prophecy of Zechariah was also an amplification of several Old Testament themes (Lk 1:67-79). If the source of the preacher's sermon is the Word of God, then it can be said that he is fulfilling a prophetic function as he preaches.

But prophecy is not the exclusive prerogative of the biblical preacher. Acts 13:1 makes it perfectly clear that there were both teachers and prophets in Antioch. Both were submissive to God's revelation as it came in the Old Testament, the teachings of Jesus, the words of Jesus given to the apostles, and the anointing of the Holy Spirit (Acts 7:2-3; Gal 1:12; 1 Jn 2:27).

The joint statement of the Evangelical Anglican Council and the Fountain Trust (England) seems best to synthesize these expressions of prophecy: "Immediacy in receiving and declaring God's present message to men is the hallmark of New Testament prophecy, as of its Old Testament counterpart. Preaching may at times approximate more to prophecy, although its basic character is one of teaching and exhortation."[6]

Regulations for New Testament Prophecy

Paul established very clear regulations regarding prophecy in the worship service. First, uncontrolled frenzy reveals that something other than the Spirit of God is being expressed in that "prophecy" (1 Cor 12:1-3). The true gift of prophecy manifests itself by the quiet spirit which is subject to the volition of the prophet (1 Cor 14:32). The prophet permits the Spirit to work, but the Spirit does not violate the person in his work. Second, only two or three prophecies are to be given at any one meeting. More than this gluts understanding and leads to dullness of hearing. Third, each prophecy is to have judgment passed on it by other prophets and leaders in the assembly (1 Cor 14:29). Fourth, the prophecy must at every point agree with the apostolic deposit or it is to be rejected (1 Cor 14:37-38). "This teaches us that the prophets were not sources of new truth to the Church, but expounders of truth otherwise revealed."[7]

Prophecy today, although it may be very helpful and on occasion overwhelmingly specific, is not in the category of the revelation given to us in Holy Scripture. Scripture is God-inspired (*theopneustos*, 2 Tim 3:16). It was superintended by God in its origination and is free of pollutants. There is no mixture of human failing with an inerrant Spirit. God's special hand was on the authors, not to override their personalities but to hedge them about in their thoughts and expressions (2 Pet 1:20-21).

Such a claim cannot be made for prophecy today. A person may hear the voice of the Lord and be compelled to speak, but there is no assurance that it is pollutant-free. There will be a mixture of both flesh and spirit. There will be a mixing of culture, personality, intellect and maturity. This should not discourage us from desiring prophetic gifts, but caution us that all prophecy must be tested, for the benefit of the body.

The accusation is often made by evangelicals that any claim to prophetic activity today undermines a high view of Scripture: Prophecy is at best neo-orthodox and at worst extrabiblical cultist dogma; if the miraculous gifts have ceased then what we see today must be fradulent.

I know of no theologically sound noncessationist who would suggest that prophecies today are inspired as Scripture is inspired of God. Strictly speaking, inspiration applies to the action of God's work with the authors of Scripture and is not used of those who prophesy.

In 1 Corinthians 14:30, however, Paul does speak of prophecy as revelation. But what type of revelation is it? Is it universal in its scope, to be obeyed by all Christians in every place and in every century? Surely not. Prophetic revelation today is different from Scripture in that it is particular rather than universal. It is a particular word, given to a particular person or group of persons, at a particular moment, for a particular purpose. Even a dispensational conservative like John F. Walvoord realizes that there is revelation for normative truth and revelation for personal direction.[8] Walvoord, however, believes that revelation for personal direction can only come by the Spirit through illumination of Scripture. But this is based on his cessationist view.

What orthodoxy has always maintained is that no direction should be taken which is counter to Scripture, not that every movement of life must have a biblical prooftext. The Spirit of God will often give guidance through circumstances, personal counsel and inward persuasion. This specific guidance does not contradict Scripture. God might also lead us through dreams, visions or prophetic words. These must be checked, of course, to see if they are contrary to Scripture, for it alone is the sole rule of doctrine and practice.

Some evangelicals have little place for the Holy Spirit today at all. They have lost the Reformational balance of the Spirit *and* the Word. Instead of being allowed to work as friends, the Spirit and the Word have been set as enemies working against each other. But Christians need both the Spirit and the Word. As Donald Gee has said, "All Word and no Spirit, we dry up. All Spirit and no Word, we blow up. With the Spirit and the Word, we grow up."

Several years ago David and Anne Watson were ministering at a large rally in our city. After a period of worship prior to David's exposition of Scripture, Anne rose and went to the microphone. Quietly and humbly she said, "I believe the Lord has given me a word for us this evening. The Lord would have us to put up our pencils and notebooks, for tonight he longs to write his words on our hearts, not our notebooks." Then she sat down and David preached. Afterwards, people came to me and said, "Where did she get that word? God used her simple word to change my life this evening!" For weeks after the meeting I received phone calls about Anne's word. A simple word, not uttered in the typical pentecostal manner nor in any way supplementing or contradicting Scripture. Yet it was a word God wanted to use in people's lives. It was a particular word for a particular moment, for a particular group of people.

Testing Prophecy in the Church
If the gift of prophecy can be legitimately exercised in the

church today, what guidelines should it follow? Three tests should be used: a theological test, a confessional test and a moral test.

Theological Test. Prophetic words are to be measured by the revelation of the Old and New Testaments (2 Tim 3:16-17; 1 Cor 14:37-38). True prophecy submits gladly to the final authority of Scripture, for it is not a new revelation of truth for the church but a harmonic expression of that truth.

John the apostle, confronting the gnostic tendencies of Cerinthus and his followers, advised the believers to test the prophets (1 Jn 4:1-3). This test was not just to get them to parrot the phrase "Jesus Christ is come in the flesh." It was to be a thorough examination of their doctrine of Christ. Therefore, we should ask of any prophetic teaching, does it agree with the apostles' testimony that Jesus Christ was fully human and fully divine? If they cannot agree with this, then Christians know that these prophets are led by the spirit of antichrist. Prophecy must be in "general agreement with scripture, and will not be accepted as adding materially to the Bible's basic revelation of God and his saving purposes in Christ."[9]

Confessional Test. First Corinthians 12:1-3 is somewhat difficult to understand because we can only conjecture about its historical context. We can be sure, however, that no word inspired by the Holy Spirit will speak disparagingly of the person and work of the Lord Jesus Christ. The words of the Spirit exalt Jesus and declare him Lord. Again, as with 1 John 4:1-3, the purpose of this test is not just to get people to parrot "Jesus is Lord." This test intends that, after first examining the theological content of the prophecy, we should listen to the spirit of the prophecy to see if we can hear in it the character of Jesus. For the Holy Spirit is the Spirit of Jesus (Jn 14:26; 2 Cor 3:17) and "the testimony of Jesus is the spirit of prophecy" (Rev 19:10).

As James Dunn has said:

> If the Spirit is by definition the Spirit of Jesus, *then Jesus himself becomes the basic criterion by which we know the Spirit.* . . .
>
> Jesus is not only the <u>risen</u> one, he is also the crucified one—the cross of Christ is as formative for Christian self-understanding as the resurrection of Christ. From which it follows that the inspiration of the Spirit of Christ is marked not just by life but also by death, not just by the power of life out of death but also by the weakness of suffering to death (2 Cor 4:7-15; 12:9-10; 13:3-4). It follows that "knowing Christ" means not only enjoying the power of his resurrection but also sharing in his suffering (Phil 3:10). A spirituality which focuses exclusively on the resurrection is as dangerously lop-sided as a spirituality which focuses exclusively on the cross.[10]

Practically, this means that we should be listening for a balance between judgment and grace in prophecy. The healing ability of Christ goes hand in hand with his aid for those who are called to endure suffering. The acceptance of sinners by Christ must be matched with Jesus' call to holiness. Singing only one tune in prophecy fails to express the full nature of Christ as it is revealed in Scripture. We should not expect that a balance of these elements will be contained in each prophecy, only that the tenor of the prophetic service, as well as the life of the congregation, will be in harmony with the full character of Jesus.

Moral Test. Jesus told us we would know false prophets by their character (Mt 7:15-20). Though outwardly equipped with proper attire and credentials, inwardly they are wolves out to destroy the sheep. Jesus calls us to be fruit inspectors, examining the lives of those who teach and prophesy to see whether the fruits of the Holy Spirit are in them (Gal 5:22-23).

Bruce Yocum accents this point:

> When we examine the statements of the New Testament

and the early church manuals in regard to discerning prophecy, we are first of all struck by the fact that they are almost exclusively concerned with discerning prophets rather than prophecies. The warnings of the epistles are directed towards false prophets, not specific false prophecies. Similarly, the *Didache* gives rules for determining whether a prophet is true or false, not whether his prophecies are true or false (11:5, 6, 12).[11]

In a community which practices relational Christianity, such testing is quite possible (Eph 4:1—6:9). But within the realm of media Christianity, globetrotting superstars, and oligarchic leadership styles, such a check is not possible. Prophecies that come through the electronic church are suspect. The viewer simply cannot investigate the character of the person who has spoken. Without a character reference, we are to remain quietly agnostic about what is said. For the same reason, churches should not let those unknown to the community share their prophetic words until the character of such persons have been proven over a period of time.

What is adequate evidence of fruitful character? We should look for spirituality which is integrated with life. Is the person "trafficking in unlived truths?" Such hypocrisy can be ruinous to the person and the community if glazed over. Second, we should look for the spirit of a servant. "Learn the lesson that, if you are to do the work of a prophet," said Bernard of Clairvaux, "what you need is not a sceptre but a hoe."[12] Is the disposition of the person to serve or to be served (Mk 10:45)? Third, we should look not only for submission to apostolic authority in Scripture, but also for submission to the leadership of the local church (1 Pet 5:5; Heb 13:17). Submission is a major sign of the Spirit-filled man or woman (Eph 5:18-21).

One additional complication concerning the regulation of prophecy applies to those who manifest various levels of emotional instability. Because of emotional sickness some should be counseled not to speak words in the name of the Lord. This need not be a permanent injunction, but it should be maintained relative to the health of the person.

Prophecy and Discernment

As the character of one giving prophecy is to be examined within the context of the community, so prophecy, given in the context of worship, is to be judged (1 Cor 14:29). Those who make the judgment are most likely fellow prophets and overseers of the church (1 Thess 5:12-22). Although a person's motives may be pure and he may have a "feeling of inspiration," there are no guarantees that the Lord indeed is speaking. So the apostles were continually reminding the churches to examine the source of the communication (1 Jn 4:1; 1 Thess 5:21).

In the Corinthian list of spiritual gifts (1 Cor 12:4-11) Paul places prophecy next to the "distinguishing of spirits" (*diakriseis pneumatōn*). *Distinguishing* of spirits finds its root in the word for judging (*diakrinō*) used in 1 Corinthians 14:29. This indicates that distinguishing of spirits is a complementary gift to prophecy as interpretation is to glossolalia.

Many commentators understand distinguishing of spirits to be the perceiving of demonic activity and exorcism.[13] No doubt this understanding has some validity. According to 1 John 4:1-3, however, what needs to be discerned is not the Spirit, but the spirit of the prophet. In the worship service, then, there is to be a discernment of the prophecies given. James Dunn argues that this subtle transference of discernment to the demonic rather than to the prophetic came about because of the neglect of the gift of prophecy. With its return to the church, we should also expect the restoration of the proper function of discernment. For, as Dunn argues,

The more highly valued a word of prophecy is by the church, the more open is that church to deception, the more liable it is to be led astray by false prophecy. Failure to recognize the role of discerning of spirits means failure to recognize the character of prophecy and prevents the gift of prophecy functioning properly. As in the worshipping assembly tongues without interpretation is in fact only half a gift, so prophecy without evaluation is in effect only half a gift.[14]

How are leaders to exercise judgment, the gift of discernment of prophecy? The context for such judgment is a *relational community* in which there is openness to confirmation as well as rebuke. Leaders must know Scripture and be able to teach and defend sound doctrine (Tit 1:9). They then must listen to hear not only the words, but the Spirit of Jesus in the prophecy. They must also ask whether the character of the person who is speaking rightly allows him or her to speak.

If these characteristics are present, the leaders should make some comment on the prophecy: Is it to be accepted or rejected by the community? Is there a Scripture to be read that shows the harmony of this prophecy with the normative revelation? Does the tone of the prophecy need to be changed? Should the person be thanked for their contribution, yet shown that the word is not of the Spirit of God? Is part of the prophecy apropos and sound while another part is polluted? Any or all of these may be used as criteria for judging a word from the Lord. And a public response should be given. Discernment does not require that all of these be used at one time, but they do provide a check list in the mind of the leadership.

Acceptable and Unacceptable Prophecy

When testing prophecy, we must be aware of the various degrees of validity and maturity in prophecy. Yocum spells these out clearly.[15] In *false prophecy,* the content and the tone are foreign to the Spirit of Jesus Christ. In *impure prophecy,* the person's own thoughts and motives are so mixed with the words from God that it is impossible to hear God speak.

A *weak prophecy* is often given by someone who is just beginning to use the prophetic gift, still has many questions about hearing God's voice and lacks the courage to submit the word to the body. Soon, however, these reservations are overcome, confidence grows and the person may now be used to give one of the following: (a) a *general word* which strengthens and warns the body, focusing on no specific person or object; (b) a *specific word* which is directed at a specific person (who may or may not be known) or concerning a specific time; (c) a *foretelling word* regarding events of the future.

Each of these three words falls under the limitation of 1 Corinthians 13:9: "For we know in part and we prophesy in part" (NIV). We are imperfect channels through which the word of God comes. Our motives and our own thinking will often cloud the communication. Therefore a person speaks with great humility and trepidation. Specific instruction to individuals—for example, when and whom to marry, what vocation to follow, what step to be taken in guidance—should be viewed with skepticism. If so specific a word is given from God, then its validity will be confirmed through other channels. As the church rediscovers the gift of prophecy, we must be willing to put up with one another's stumbling and inadequate attempts to share God's word. All gifts come to us in latent form and must be developed. This is true also with those who prophesy.

Preparations for the Gift of Prophecy
In preparation for weekly Bible exposition, I spend at least one half of each week preparing to teach. Those who have

prophetic gifts will find the disciplines and preparation no less demanding, though they may have less time than I do to devote to ministry. To prophesy does not make you a prophet, but it does enroll you in the stretching school of prophets. Here are a few necessary disciplines for those who wish to exercise this gift.

Saturation in Scripture. The gift of prophecy flows out of the heart of Scripture. It is the concerns of Scripture which God will place on your heart to give to other people. Often it will simply be the use of an appropriate Scripture which is "in season" for the person's need. Other times it will be a picture or vision which is stimulated by biblical words, parables or analogies. Only those who have pored over and digested Scripture are fully prepared for prophecy.

Fasting. Periodic abstensions from food (not water) and sexual activity (Mt 6:16-18; 1 Cor 7:5) heighten one's sense for kingdom priorities. During these periods attention is turned away from the physical maintenance of life so that one's priorities can be attuned to prayer and meditation.[16]

Worship. As Isaiah did not "go and tell" without first encountering the transcendent holiness of God (6:1-13), so prophets today must first meet God in his holiness. Cleansed lips beget praise and preparation for divine service.

Waiting Prayer. In the presence of God one need not always be speaking. Quietly we may sing the articulate choruses of the living creatures (Rev 7:11-12) or sing in an unknown song of the Spirit (1 Cor 14:15). But mostly we should be quiet. Soon the "inner voice" of the Spirit will give the direction necessary for edification, exhortation or consolation. Expectant faith is needed in the season of silence. God loves his children and wants them to know and possess everything needed for life and godliness. If a word is needed for someone, we can be assured that God wants to give it.

Recollection. During waiting periods, write out the words that God has given. Time quickly erases the train of thought that was so fresh at the moment. Diaries of dreams, visions and words reduce our tendency to overstate or forget.

Courage. A relationship with God's Holy Spirit is not like an automatic pilot on an airplane. We do not just let go and let him do all the work. God's Spirit is always working hand in hand with us to help us over the rough spots of life and ministry (Rom 8:26-28). We need to rely on the Holy Spirit for the courage to speak, for as soon as we open our lips we will feel that we are on our own and that the next word is uncharted territory. Despite the fright we must go on. God's words will be there for those who are listening at every moment and have the courage to speak.

November 12

Finding appropriate housing in our area of the country is a very discouraging venture. Members of our Christian community, nevertheless, encouraged us to begin looking for a house to purchase. A realtor friend consented to tour us around the neighborhood showing what was available. The first house we drove by was a delightful, three-bedroom bungalow with an immaculately kept garden. That was the good news. The bad news was that the house had five full cash offers and there seemed to be no way for us to get it. After one hour of driving we packed it in for the day. My wife and I confessed that night, "Only the Lord can find a house for us!"

A few days later, during the second week of October, our seven-year-old daughter sensed our discouragement. At dinner that evening she looked at my wife and me and said, "Don't be discouraged, Daddy. God has told me we will have our house on November 12!" Like a good evangelical parent I welcomed her optimism but cautioned her about date setting in the name of God. I also told her to be careful lest she believe something which later turned out to be false. Undaunted, she returned to dinner the next night with a repeat of the same message. At this point I began to ponder these things in my heart (Lk 2:51).

As the weeks went on, there seemed to be no time for house hunting. Yet as November 12 approached I began to sense a great deal of excitement. I was sufficiently prudent, however, not to tell anyone of my daughter's prediction. The day finally arrived. After lunch I casually dropped by my realtor's office. "Did you receive my phone call?" asked Barry. "What call?" I answered. Barry went on to explain that he had tried to reach me thirty minutes before to tell me that the little three-bedroom bungalow, because of legal complications, had gone off the market for several weeks and had just that moment been placed back on again. Immediately I phoned a friend and we rushed to the house and made an offer, an offer which was accepted on the afternoon of November 12, 1980.

Eryn Faye and her mother had often spoken to one another of hearing God's voice in guidance. God's direction in our purchase of a house was just one of many things God wants to do in our family. This account is a fitting conclusion to what has been said about prophecy. Perhaps it will serve to heighten our expectation that God can and does speak to his children.

3
Dreams and Visions: God's Picture Language
John Opmeer

In the year 390 Ambrose, bishop of Milan, wrote a letter to the Roman Emperor Theodosius in which he called him to public repentance for ordering a massacre in Thessalonica. In this bold and now famous letter, Ambrose declared that God had warned him in a dream not to celebrate communion before the Emperor unless Theodosius repented. These are his words:

> I am writing with my own hand that which you alone may read. . . . I have been warned, not by man, nor through man, but plainly by Himself that this is forbidden me. For when I was anxious, in the very night in which I was preparing to set out, you appeared to me in a dream to have come into the Church, and I was not permitted to offer the sacrifice. . . . Our God gives warnings in many ways, by heavenly signs, by the precepts of the prophets; by the visions even of sinners He wills that we should understand, that we should entreat Him to take away all disturbances . . . that the faith and peace of the Church . . . may continue![1]

How many Christians today would risk position, and even

life, to carry out a command of God given in a dream? Yet, for some three thousand years God's people gave dreams this kind of weight. The moment we step into their world, we are amazed at the utter confidence people had in the message that came to them from God through a dream or vision.

In the Bible, from Genesis to Revelation, dreams and visions abound. After reading Scripture, a person unfamiliar with church history would certainly expect dreams and visions to be a normal means of encounter with God. But we do not see this happening today in the church. Dreams and visions suffer such an anemic reputation that John Sanford has called them "God's forgotten language."[2]

In the secular marketplace it is different. Ever since Freud and Jung there has been a fascination with dreams and visions in psychology and anthropology, as well as in popular magazines, books and movies.

How can a subject that is so well publicized in Scripture and endowed with such glorious promises have become so unfamiliar and unloved, treated with suspicion, and thought of as less than the stepchild of theology? When we find answers to this question, we may also recover the confidence with which people like Ambrose spoke when God communicated with them through dreams and visions.

Dreamers and Visionaries
Turning to the Old Testament, we are met by an impressive list of dreamers and visionaries, two of whom are Jacob and Daniel.

After tricking his father and taking his brother Esau's birthright, Jacob went through a severe crisis. He fled from the wrath of Esau (Gen 28). At the end of his first day as a fugitive, Jacob fell asleep in the open field and dreamed about angels going up and down a ladder to heaven. He also heard God's promise to give to him and his descendants the land on which he slept. The memory of this dream shaped Jacob's life and the history of Israel.

Daniel's dreams are as personal as Jacob's, but their frame of reference is even larger. In them God is dealing with the future of Israel and the nations. In Daniel 2 we find him interpreting a dream of King Nebuchadnezzar in which a mighty image of various metals is smashed by a small stone. Daniel's own dreams are recorded in the later chapters. They also deal with the future, all the way to the end of human history. These visions were so powerful in their effect on Daniel, that they left him physically weak for days (7:28; 8:27; 10:16).

Varieties of Dreams and Visions

Two kinds of dreams may be distinguished in the Old Testament. First, there are "ordinary" dreams in which the sleeper sees a connected series of images which correspond to events in everyday life, such as the chief butler's and chief baker's dreams (Gen 40:9-17). Second, dreams may simply communicate a message from God, either directly or through angels, such as when God spoke to Abimelech about Abraham's wife Sarah (Gen 20:3-7). A vision usually occurs to someone who is awake, often during the night (Gen 46:2; Zech 4:1-2). Visions, like dreams, can be distinguished into those which relate to the visible world (for example, Amos 7:1-3; 8:1, 2; Jer 1:11-12), and others in which the invisible is made visible, such as those found frequently in Ezekiel and Daniel. Ordinarily, only prophets would see the "other" reality. But there were exceptions, such as Elisha's servant, who saw the heavenly armies after his master had prayed, "LORD,...open his eyes, that he may see" (2 Kings 6:17).

Joel's Pentecost Prophecy

Gerhard von Rad has pointed out that there is no instance

in the Old Testament where a vision is not immediately followed by the Word of God.[3] This may explain why visions were a more honored means of divine communication than were dreams. The presence or absence of visions in Israel became an indicator of spiritual condition. When Israel was unfaithful, the prophets lamented the absence of visions from the Lord. Said Jeremiah, "The law is no more, and her prophets obtain no vision from the LORD" (Lam 2:9). The Lord promised, however, that a day would come when visions would be restored to God's people. The most famous of these prophecies is Joel 2:28:

And it shall come to pass afterward,
> that I will pour out my spirit on all flesh;
your sons and your daughters shall prophesy,
> your old men shall dream dreams,
> and your young men shall see visions.

The prophet Joel, himself a dreamer and visionary, speaks here of a distant age in which God would pour out his Spirit on his people everywhere. Joel is saying at least three things in this prophecy.

First, in the coming age the anointing of the Holy Spirit will not be limited to kings, prophets and judges. It will be given to all God's people, without differentiation of office, class, age or sex. It is likely that Joel understood "all flesh" to refer to the house of Israel.

Second, the visual and aural proof of the new promise of the Spirit in God's people will be the gift of prophecy. Moses' wish "that all the LORD's people were prophets" (Num 11:29) will come to fulfillment. Dreams and visions are assigned a place of honor among the various ways in which God makes known his will to believers.

Third, Joel's prophecy deals with a time of restoration of the fortunes of Israel and of judgment on the nations (Joel 3:1-2). If we did not have the inspired interpretation of the New Testament text, we almost would have to conclude that the prophecy had not been fulfilled yet!

New Testament Fulfillment

Several centuries after Joel, at the Jewish feast of Pentecost, the apostle Peter made the dramatic announcement that Joel's prophecy was being fulfilled that day. The phenomena that perplexed a large gathering of Jewish-pilgrims in Jerusalem that morning are explained with the words, "This is what was spoken by the prophet Joel" (Acts 2:16). What was Peter saying?

First, with the outpouring of the Holy Spirit on the followers of Jesus, the last days preceding the day of the Lord had arrived. The age of the Spirit, now ushered in, would continue until all the events prophesied by Joel, including the destruction of Israel's enemies and the cosmic disturbances, take place.

Second, Peter had an amazing liberty to go beyond the traditional association between Joel's prophecy and the restoration of the fortunes of Israel. On that day Peter did not yet realize the full implication of the words "all flesh." But it was not long before he did. Before many weeks had passed, God—through a vision—had convinced Peter to abandon his "for Jews only" mentality. Following Peter, all the other apostles understood that the fulfillment of Joel's prophecy had universal application (1 Cor 12:13; Gal 3:28; Rev 7:9).

Third, Peter's reference to dreams, visions and prophecies as marks of the new era of the Spirit is important. There had been no mention of dreams and visions in Jesus' ministry with the Twelve. Yet on that Pentecost morning, Peter associated these phenomena with the new presence of the Spirit prophesied by Joel. They are *signs* of the presence of the Spirit, as well as *tools* in the work of ministry needed for the guidance and growth of the followers of Jesus Christ.

A Gap in New Testament Theology

Not surprisingly, then, when we read the book of Acts, we find that dreams and visions played a major and fascinating role in the life of the emerging Christian church. The infant church, unencumbered by modern scientific presuppositions, expected and received guidance from God.

Turning directly from the New Testament to modern New Testament theology, we are shocked to find that the subject of dreams and visions is largely ignored by New Testament theologians. Alan Richardson's *Theological Word Book of the Bible* has no entry for "dreams."[4] Under the heading "visions" we read that for the most part the New Testament interest is confined to the Lukan writings, whereas Paul did not set much store by visionary experiences.[5] Not a word on the implications of Joel's prophecy for New Testament church life.

According to Merrill Unger, "In the era of an outpoured Spirit and a full written revelation to guide, we walk by faith, and normally have little need for such unusual methods of guidance."[6] This seems like Joel 2:28 in reverse! What has happened? Faith has been identified with the written revelation, and sight with dreams and visions.

But we look in vain for such a contrast in the New Testament, and Unger's "unusual methods of guidance" seem rather common there. The apostles knew that Joel had not prophesied, "You *apostles* shall see visions." A new day had arrived. What was unusual before had now become usual. The Old Testament pattern of dreams and visions for only a few would not be continued. Now, ordinary believers, even those low on the social ladder, would dream dreams through which God would communicate with his people. Now, prophecy would be heard in every local gathering of believers.

In order to understand the contrast between the New Testament and current versions of New Testament theology on dreams and visions, we need to retrace the steps of the church from the close of the apostolic period forward to the present.

The Postapostolic Period
With the death of the last apostle, there was no sudden lapse of dreams and visions. Nor did the church become dreamless as soon as it had settled the question of the New Testament canon. The historic record does not support such dispensational thinking. Instead, the history of this period reads almost like a sequel to the book of Acts. If a Who's Who of the early church had been compiled, it would have included an impressive number of dreamers and visionaries in the Joel tradition.

The aged Polycarp, on his way to martyrdom in Rome, dreamed that he would be burned alive.[7] Irenaeus, bishop of Lyons in the latter part of the second century, commented extensively on the biblical passages on dreams and visions, emphasizing the function of dreams in conveying the likeness of God's nature even though God himself is invisible.[8] Origen, one of the greatest thinkers of the third century, stressed the importance of dreams and visions as means of revelation in his writings.[9]

Tertullian, the great Latin scholar and contemporary of Origen, made a special study of dreams. He wrote in *A Treatise on the Soul,* "Almost the greater part of mankind get their knowledge of God from dreams." It was Tertullian's conviction that dreams are a gift from God.[10]

Cyprian, the great third-century bishop of Carthage in North Africa, looked to his dreams for practical guidance in making decisions. In one letter, concerning the granting of pardon to lapsed Christians, he notes that he and his colleagues have been guided by the Holy Spirit by "many and manifest visions." In another letter, discussing the ordination of a certain Celerinus, he makes special mention of the guidance Celerinus received "in a vision by night."[11]

Augustine (354-430), who laid the intellectual foundation for Western Christian thinking for at least a millennium, placed great emphasis on dreams and visions as a continuing means of revelation and guidance. He believed that dreams and visions do not reveal the nature of God, but are examples of his providential care and his gifts.[12]

Jerome, a contemporary of Augustine, is known best for his translation of the Bible into Latin, the so-called Vulgate translation. What is less known is that his life was completely altered by a dream. As a classical scholar and a nominal Christian, he had a dream in which he saw himself standing before the judgment seat of God. He stated that he was a Christian. But the Judge responded: "Thou liest, thou art a follower of Cicero and not of Christ!" As a result of this dream, Jerome dedicated the rest of his life to the study of Scripture. He wrote much on the subject of dreams and visions, showing their use by God, and yet warning against seeking them for their own sake.[13]

Morton Kelsey, in whose book *God, Dreams, and Revelation* much of the above material is discussed, deserves credit for his efforts to unearth a wealth of documentation on dreams and visions from this period of church history. Kelsey mentions many other writers of the ante- and post-Nicene church who wrote positively about dreams and visions.[14]

It must not be concluded from the names listed so far that only prominent church leaders were dreamers and visionaries at that time. But being writers, their experiences were more likely to be recorded and preserved for posterity. The tradition of respect for dreams and visions as channels of revelation was kept intact in the Eastern wing of the church via such leaders as Gregory of Nyssa and Basil the Great. Much of this tradition has been preserved to the present in the Eastern Orthodox churches. In the Western church, however, a different development took place.

The Fading of the Vision

For five centuries the church accepted the phenomena mentioned by Joel as normal signs of the new age of the Spirit. Then, slowly, they began to fade. Several factors are responsible for this development.

First, through the growing political power of the bishops, they were increasingly seen as intermediaries between God and the people. Emphasis on direct communication of the "laity" with God declined. James Ash, who has studied the decline of prophecy in the early church, concludes that the institutionalization of the church was accompanied by the disappearance of prophetic activities in the church at large. Ash documents from early sources a clear trend towards a monopoly of all charismatic activity by the bishops.[15]

Second, an unfortunate mistranslation by the great scholar Jerome contributed to the growing distrust of dreams. Jerome translated Leviticus 19:26 and Deuteronomy 18:10 "You shall not practice augury nor observe dreams."[16] The NIV has "Do not practice divination or sorcery." Thus, by the authority of the Vulgate, which was practically the only Bible in the Western church until the Reformation, Christians had no choice but to suspect dreams as a form of soothsaying!

Third, with the collapse of the Roman Empire, the West entered the so-called Dark Ages, which were marked by much superstition. The church was not free from this, and its leaders found it necessary to emphasize more and more the scriptural caution on the matter of dreams and visions (Jer 23:28-29). Following Gregory the Great (sixth century), who was torn between acceptance and rejection of dreams, the church for the next six hundred years increasingly hesitated to accept the value of visual or aural prophecy.

The crowning blow to the respectability of dreams and visions was delivered by Thomas Aquinas. During his time, the Greek philosopher Aristotle, who had become quite popular in the West, was adopted by church scholars. Aristotle, in contrast to Plato, had no use for dreams and visions, since he believed that human knowledge is derived only from the physical senses and human reason. Aquinas was the first to fully integrate Aristotelian thought with Christian theology. Although he struggled for a while to make sense of Numbers 12:6 ("If there is a prophet among you, I the LORD make myself known to him in a vision, I speak with him in a dream"), in the end, as Kelsey puts it, "the philosopher won and the Bible lost."[17]

The irony is that Thomas Aquinas, the "doctor angelicus" who is responsible for so much of the present disregard of the dreams and visions in Joel's end-time prophecy, disclaimed his own views toward the end of his life. The doctor who had no use for visions, himself received a vision of God. After that, he refused to write and dictate. When he was urged to go on, he replied, "I can do no more; such things have been revealed to me that all I have written seems as straw, and now I await the end of my life." Unfortunately, the church kept the straw and forgot the vision.[18]

Some Notable Exceptions

Visions were never completely forgotten, of course. In spite of the protests of the church, suspicion, ridicule and even persecution, dreamers and visionaries continued to be found in the church. Many, if not most of the revival movements, were accompanied by some charismatic phenomena, including dreams and visions.[19] Documentation is rather limited, due in part, no doubt, to the unsympathetic bias of those who wrote the histories. Occasionally, however, the critics supply the information themselves, as is the case with the anonymous article entitled "The Wonderful, Wandering Spirit" (1741) which ridiculed the "excesses" of the Great Awakening.[20]

And, in spite of the stigma attached to dreams and visions, several respected Protestants have reported dreams from their own experience. John Newton, for example, the author of "Amazing Grace," tells in his autobiography that years before his conversion God warned him in a dream of the danger of his way of life. In the dream, he was given a ring that would bring happiness. He promised the giver he would take care of the ring. A second person managed to make him doubt the ring, however, and he threw it overboard. Immediately, mountains in the distance burst into flames. Newton understood that he had thrown away the mercy of God.

As the dream continued, the first person returned, rebuked him for his rashness and recovered the ring from the sea. He refused to give it back to Newton. Instead, he offered to keep it for him and to produce it on his behalf whenever needed. Newton forgot the dream soon afterwards, but years later found himself in circumstances resembling the situation of the dream. This led to his conversion.[21]

One name that should not be left out is that of Charles Finney, the evangelist who led many to Christ during half a century of revival preaching. He was launched into an evangelistic career by a mighty baptism of the Holy Spirit which he experienced in 1821 through a remarkable vision of Christ. Nor was this his only vision. In his autobiography, Finney recalls a number of visions which he received, usually at times of strong persecution against him.[22]

By and large, the institutional church, particularly the Protestant and evangelical communions, have considered dreams and visions the products of an overheated imagination. For practical purposes, Joel's prophecy was a thing of

61

the past, a half-buried memory. It would take a mighty movement of God's Spirit to restore faith in dreams and visions as manifestations of the era of the Spirit.

The Twentieth Century

By God's grace, the twentieth century is witnessing that movement. We are seeing a renewal of some neglected manifestations of the Spirit. First in the pentecostal revival and now in the charismatic renewal of the second half of the century, dreams and visions and other spiritual phenomena are returning to the heart of the church's life.

In 1936, the British evangelist Smith Wigglesworth was guest of the young General Secretary of the Apostolic Faith Mission of South Africa, David du Plessis. At 7 A.M. one morning, Wigglesworth walked into du Plessis's office and began to tell him of visions he had been seeing that morning. God had told him that he would bring a mighty renewal to the churches in the last days, compared to which the pentecostal movement would be a mere beginning. David du Plessis would have to bring the message of this pentecost to all churches. He would travel more than most evangelists do. The vision would come to pass after he, Smith Wigglesworth, had died.

That was the message. Up to that time, David du Plessis had never been outside South Africa. On March 12, 1947, Smith Wigglesworth died. The same year, du Plessis began his travels, which were to take him to the historic churches, including the Roman Catholic Church (for pentecostals, the "scarlet woman" of the book of Revelation). The prophecy was fulfilled to the letter. David du Plessis has traveled over a million miles so far. In the fifties, the prophecy of a renewal in the historic churches began to come true. David du Plessis is now known the world over as "Mr. Pentecost."[23]

The subject can no longer be ignored, or dismissed on

the charge of theological naiveté or excessive emotion. A change is occurring in both theology and experience. Thousands upon thousands of Christians, including outstanding leaders and mature believers, have testified that God has guided them and the church through dreams and visions. David Wilkerson, of Teen Challenge, Demos Shakarian, of the Full Gospel Businessmen's Fellowship, and Harold Bredesen, one of the charismatic pioneers, are just a few.[24]

But Joel's prophecy speaks of ordinary believers as candidates for the manifestations of the Spirit. Victor Landero, a humble farmer in the tiny village of Corozalito, Colombia, South America, is a good example. Victor had a strong desire to evangelize. One night he dreamed about a house in the forest. It was an ordinary house, but he had never seen that particular one before. He heard a voice saying, "The people in that house are dying without Christ because no one ever told them of him." Victor heard that same voice several more times during the next few months, but he dismissed the dream from his mind as not important.

Finally, after eight months, Victor told the Lord that he was willing to tell those people of Christ, if God would show him where to go. He took a companion and went to look for the house. About noon on the second day, there stood the house, in a clearing in the woods, exactly as Victor had seen it in his dreams.

The woman who came out as he approached was astounded when she heard Victor's request for a meeting that night in her house. She had already seen him in a dream, three days earlier, standing in her home, with people jammed in wall to wall. That night, all twenty-four of the neighbors who had come received Christ. The next night, they all returned with ten more. At the end of that night, there were thirty-four new believers in Christ.

David Howard, a former Inter-Varsity Christian Fellowship missions director, who tells the story, visited that little village a year later. By that time there were about fifty Christians. He writes, "The fact that God used a dream to accomplish this should not be surprising. If he gave Peter a vision prior to leading him to Cornelius, and if he gave Cornelius a vision to tell him to send for Peter (see Acts 10) ... why can he not do that today in Colombia if he so chooses?"[25] Indeed. How very *un*surprising given that God served notice through Joel that he would make use of these means in the new age of the Spirit.

Dreams from the Spirit?

But *which* dreams are a fulfillment of Joel's prophecy? Humans have always dreamed. What is so different about the age of the Holy Spirit? Non-Christians dream as often as Christians. Many, if not most of our dreams have emotional and physical causes, such as worry, fear, desire, exhaustion, sickness or medication.

In the Old Testament there is recognition of various sources of dreams and visions. In Ecclesiastes 5:6 dreams are explained psychologically—springing from the restless human mind. And Jeremiah warned that the dreams and visions of false prophets are mere straw (Jer 14:14; 23:28-29).

So what assurance do we have that Christians' dreams are different? Does the presence of the Holy Spirit really have any special relevance to the dreams and visions of Christians? And if so, are we talking about dreams in general, or about a special kind of dream that is of a revelatory nature?

Any kind of insight is "revelatory" in a way. But unless we establish beyond a doubt that the outpouring of the Holy Spirit makes a difference in this matter, we end up with not-so-sanctified confusion and warmed-over psychology served as a special treat of the Spirit.

Why God Uses Dreams and Visions

Another question comes to mind: Why is it that God chooses

to make use of dreams and visions at all?

First of all, because the conscious mind—even of the believer—is not always fully receptive to the Spirit of God. Fears, preconceived ideas, carnality and other elements may block or distort the reception of God's message. Because they come to us apart from or perhaps despite the controlled and conscious mind, dreams and visions have a way of cancelling out the "static" caused by the mind of the recipient.

Second, as we all know, a picture is worth a thousand words. Whereas nonvisual means of revelation may not succeed in getting the message across, pictures freely, effectively and immediately communicate.

Third, since dreams and visions are not limited to the physical, God can use them to give his prophets access to another realm of reality.

Fourth, pictures are well-suited to reveal and yet hide at the same time, allowing God to make known a message that will become meaningful only at a later time.

Often visions have been used by God to get attention. First, there is the vision; then the message (Amos 8:1-2; Zech 1—6).

Of the two means of visual prophecy, dreams involve the least interference from the conscious mind. For that reason, the dream may be called God's elementary language to all people. Visions are received while awake and are thus more subject to control. Apart from this, little distinction need be made between dreams and visions. Time and again, these two means of visual revelation are mentioned together in the Old Testament (Dan 7:1; Num 12:6; Job 4:13; Is 29:7).

The Lord Communicator

We return to the question, Are the dreams of Christians any different from the dreams of the rest of society? If we start with Joel's prophecy, his reference seems to be to a special kind of dream; namely, those dreams that have as their frame of reference, not the private life of an individual, but the expression of God's will and purpose for his people and the world. Occasionally, the subject may be the life of just one person, but even then the background is the covenant community of Israel. Since in all of Scripture dreams and visions are closely related to prophecy, we may take it for granted that this is what Joel had in mind: visual prophecy in its full biblical range, both predictive (as in Amos 3:7) and edifying (as in 1 Cor 14:3-4).

Furthermore, dreams and visions are closely connected with all the gifts of the Spirit mentioned in the New Testament. A word of knowledge came through a vision (Acts 27:23-26). So did a gift of healing (Acts 9:10-12) and of evangelism (Acts 8:26). Possibly the reason that dreams and visions are not listed with the charismata in the New Testament is that they are included under the various gifts, particularly under prophecy. All these gifts are given for the express purpose of relating the Christian community more closely to Jesus Christ, to his mind, grace, power and calling. The Holy Spirit relates to non-Christians mostly by way of conviction of sin, of righteousness and of judgment (Jn 16:8). Dreams and visions may be channels used by God to relate to unbelievers in a providential way. But the indwelling Spirit communicates more directly with Christians, to guide them into all truth (Jn 16:13). Therefore, dreams and visions are signs of the presence of the Holy Spirit whenever they strengthen, comfort, guide and warn believers, or more generally build up the church in its preaching, fellowship and service.

It will be difficult, if not impossible, to prove rationally whether a dream has been given by the Spirit or has arisen out of our own subconscious mind. At least certain dreams and visions *are* given by God and as such they are prophetic in nature and gifts of the Spirit to the church. There is no need for us to agonize which is which. A Christian is by definition one who is controlled by the Spirit (Rom 8:9). This control includes the subconscious mind. We can say, therefore, that Joel's prophecy is fulfilled in the life of every born-again Christian.

The ability to receive prophetic messages and images from the Lord, however, is not equal among all Christians. We may think of such ability in terms of a sliding scale. We do not even have to limit our observations to Christians. Many non-Christians are sensitive of spirit and are open to God as they perceive him. Scripture teaches us that God graciously seeks to communicate with all people, and that his ability to do so increases with the level and content of a person's faith (Rom 1:20; 2:18-20; 1 Cor 2:14-16). Believers in God as Creator only are less open to God's mind than those who believe in him as Creator and Redeemer. Nominal Christians often have a knowledge of the Bible that is greater than that of adherents of other faiths, but yet they may be less open to the Spirit of God. And all of these will be less discerning of the Spirit's voice than those who are born of the Spirit: the recipients of the outpoured Holy Spirit of which Joel spoke. Common believers—educated and uneducated alike—may, and do, receive prophetic dreams and visions. And again there is a sliding scale. Some believers receive a gift of prophecy that is so outstanding that they are called prophets. Others may be especially filled with the Spirit (Acts 6:3, 8). We do not need a pentecostal theology in order to appreciate this simple fact. Rather, in a humble way we must recognize that, for whatever reasons, some Christians are apparently more filled with the Spirit, or more often so, than other Christians. We may say, then, that the more open a person is to the Spirit of Jesus, the more he or she will be able to hear what the Spirit is saying.

One of our sons, after three years of study at the University of British Columbia, was unsure whether to return for his fourth year that fall or to take a year off for work or travel. I had suggested the possibility of going to Bible school for a year, but none of these options really appealed to him.

One evening in late summer, frustrated with his indecision, he prayed earnestly for direction. In his daily Bible reading he happened to be at James 1. He saw verses 5-7 and was greatly encouraged. Faith was given to him that he would have a definite answer in a dream.

The next morning he woke up at 6:30 and prayed, "Lord, I did not have my dream yet!" He then fell asleep again and dreamed that he was walking down a school hallway with a friend. Together, they were carrying a huge watermelon. Somehow it slipped from their hands and cracked open on the floor. Out of the crack emerged three words: Christian Center, Anaheim. The dream was vivid in his memory when he woke up again. The thought came to him: God gave me an answer; whatever it means, will I commit myself to that answer? He decided to commit himself to follow the direction given.

The words "Christian Center, Anaheim," however, were not clear to him. Without telling the dream, he asked my wife if she knew of a Christian Center in Anaheim. She told him that there was one in California called Melodyland. Only then did he tell about the dream. He was not excited at all about going to a Bible school, but decided to go for a year out of obedience to the guidance given. The first few months were difficult. Then he picked up interest, and stayed for a second year to get a bachelor's degree.

Insights gained day by day by Christians through dreams and visions are part of the normal life in Christ. God may choose to guide us through a dream, whether we think of that dream as just a dream or a prophetic dream. Our overall conclusion to the question whether the presence of the Holy Spirit makes any difference with respect to dreams and visions is, then, that indeed there is a marvelous difference. The promise of dreams and visions in the age of the Spirit is fulfilled in the greatly heightened capacity of Christians to understand the mind and the will of God.

The Interpretation of Dreams

The difference the Holy Spirit makes in the matter of dreams and visions includes the area of interpretation. "Do not interpretations belong to God?" (Gen 40:8).

If a dream or vision has been given by God, he should have, so to speak, the exclusive right of interpretation. A dream is nothing without its interpretation. If the source of a dream is not in our minds, we cannot be trusted to discover its meaning. This is true of dreams and visions given to Christians, and certainly also of those given to non-Christians. If we take the Bible as our guide, we know that unbelievers are not excluded by God in this area. Significant messages were entrusted by God at times to those outside of the covenant community of Israel. But they usually did not understand the message until someone interpreted it for them, someone who had been given the gift of interpretation by God. Some well-known examples are Joseph to Pharaoh (Gen 41), Daniel to king Nebuchadnezzar (Dan 2 and 4), and Daniel to king Belshazzar (Dan 5). Seldom was the interpreter a person without explicit faith in the God of Israel.

Such interpretation was expected in Israel from those particularly anointed with the Spirit of Yahweh. Joel foresaw a time in which all believers would be potential interpreters.

Not all insight is hidden from non-Christians. Particularly in the area of private dreams great interpretative expertise has been developed over the years, beginning with

Freud. We may expect, however, that those who have received the Spirit of Jesus are more likely to be able to give an interpretation of a dream or vision sent by God than those who have not the Spirit of Christ. The gift of interpretation is as much a charisma of the Spirit in the church as the gift of wisdom or of knowledge. The Holy Spirit is the Master Interpreter.

Warnings in Dreams

Sometimes people dream about events that have not happened yet. The apostle Paul declared to the elders in Ephesus, "The Holy Spirit testifies to me in every city that imprisonment and afflictions await me" in Jerusalem (Acts 20:23). This conviction came to him through words of knowledge or visions granted to him and several other believers. Such messages may be given as foreknowledge or as a warning.

Polycarp's dream, while he was imprisoned, that he would be burned alive was foreknowledge. Alexander the Great, intending to sack Jerusalem, was warned in a dream not to harm the Jews. As a result, he spared Jerusalem and actually knelt before the Jewish high priest. The American president Abraham Lincoln saw his body lying in state in the White House. If this dream was given as a warning, it was not heeded: a few days later, Lincoln was assassinated.

Safeguards

Just as we need a new openness and sensitivity toward dreams and visions, we also need safeguards in dealing with them in the church. Dreams and visions reflect our own inner life, and some of that life cannot be trusted. The promise is that those who are filled with the Spirit will get the clearest messages from God. Mere human elements play larger roles in our dreams to the extent that we consciously or unconsciously do not allow the Holy Spirit to have control. If our subconscious is not at all committed to God, our dreams will be largely a product of our flesh.

Our dreams and visions, therefore, may have either a human or a divine source, or both. Certainly there is a difference between these two sources, but often we are not able to distinguish one from the other. Morton Kelsey observes, "I wonder if this inner voice is not the action of the Holy Spirit."[26] To evangelical ears this may sound suspicious, but Scripture teaches that the Holy Spirit is able to communicate with unbelievers, warning them about the consequences of a life without God (Jn 16:8).

Since there will almost always be this ambivalence about the source of dreams or visions, we need tests. And all the more so because some dreams have a supernatural origin that is not of God. Satan, the master counterfeiter, has invaded this area and desires to lead people astray. The Bible warns us against false dreams (Jer 14:14; Ezek 13:3-7).

How are we to know that a dream is really sent by God? How should we respond to those who claim, "Last night the Lord told me in a dream . . . " or who, during a prayer meeting, say, "I see a vision of . . ."? How do we know that this is indeed of the Lord? How do *they* know? It could be a case of sincere but wishful thinking. It could be an unconscious effort on their part to sound spiritual. In short, how do we prevent an opening of the floodgates of subjectivism or infiltration by enemy forces?

First, does the message agree with Scripture? That is, does it agree with the text of Scripture, sound doctrine and established Christian principles? Does the dream, for example, prepare for a time of testing? Does it point out sins or problem areas? Does it built up, encourage or comfort (1 Cor 14:1)?

Joseph Smith, founder of the Church of Latter-day Saints, may have had visions. But they were not of God, since they contradicted the doctrine of the authority of

Scripture and the doctrine of God, to mention only two. Mormonism is dependent on the false visions of Joseph Smith. The same can be said of Christian Science, whose founder, Mary Baker Eddy, taught that sin and death are mere illusions. On the other hand, John Newton's dream, as we have seen, warned him not to neglect the grace of God and was therefore in keeping with Scripture.

Second, does the vision or dream draw us closer to the true God, to Jesus Christ? Parallel to this, does it lead to peace in doing God's will, or to panic, fear or depression? The factual accuracy of the dream does not alone constitute evidence of divine origin. Deuteronomy 13:1-5 warns against prophets whose words come to pass, but who say, "Let us go after other gods."

Third, does the recipient of the dream or vision have occult contacts? The involvement may be current (a number of so-called born-again Christians visit spiritualist churches), or in the past, but not repented of. "Test the spirits" (1 Jn 4:1-3).

The late Bishop Pike, after the death of his son, tried to establish contact with him via a medium. Apparently, at one seance he saw an apparition of his son and was reassured by him. Such a vision cannot be of God, because it came via an occult contact, in disobedience of Deuteronomy 18:10-11.

Fourth, does the message exalt the receiver or the giver? We should be wary when a dream or vision is seen as a sign of spirituality. In some prayer groups and charismatic contexts it seems as if a word from Scripture has less standing than a word through a special prophecy (Col 2:18-19). Such groups often start with genuine visions from the Lord, but then slip into the error of seeking visions for their own sake.

Fifth, wait for confirmation through other means, if at all possible. Harold Bredesen recounts a large number of remarkable dreams and visions in his book *Yes, Lord.* Some time before he received a call from the historic Dutch Reformed Church in Mt. Vernon, New York, a friend phoned him to tell of a vision she had of Bredesen preaching in a church. She described the church building in detail, with the grounds around it, and the parsonage. Neither she nor Bredesen had ever seen this building. When Bredesen was called to this church, he recognized the building as the one his friend had seen in her vision.[27] The call was accepted, but not on the basis of the vision. According to Bredesen, it is best not to take action based *solely* on visions.

Sixth, submit a dream or vision to the counsel of trusted Christians, especially when it calls for action. If the setting of the vision is a prayer meeting, ask for prayer at the meeting, for testing and interpretation. The Holy Spirit is the interpreter par excellence, and he will help to discern the source and the purpose of the communication, through the body of Christ.

Several Christians who have shared dreams with me have expressed their fear that Satan might be behind the dream. As a general rule, and keeping in mind the tests that can be applied, Christians do not have to entertain such doubts. If we have sincerely confessed Jesus Christ and submitted our life to his lordship, then he is Lord also over our dream life. We may trust that he will protect us from false dreams and visions or will give us the discernment to distinguish what is from God and what is not.

The Holy Spirit: Our Interpreter

Most dreams and visions need interpretation. Although we may learn from the studies of psychologists in this area, God is our interpreter. As Joseph said to the cupbearer and baker in prison, "Do not interpretations belong to God?" (Gen 40:8). We should therefore always ask God for help in understanding a dream or vision.

To benefit from our own dreams or to help others with

theirs does not require us to become dream experts. Most dreams make sense only against a background of the dreamer's circumstances and past. Interpretation usually is not arrived at by logical analysis or study of books, but by way of a sudden realization or insight, an "Aha!" experience like Peter's. In Cornelius' house, four days after his rooftop vision, he suddenly understood his vision: "I perceive that God shows no partiality" (Acts 10:34).

Once you are open to the possibility that God may speak to you and are willing to take dreams and visions seriously, what should you do?

First, and most important, surrender this part of your life to God. Ask him to protect you from false sources, and to help you learn to be sensitive to what for you is an unfamiliar channel of communication.

Second, learn to remember your dreams. This is not easy. Ninety-five per cent of dreams are forgotten within five minutes of waking. A dream that is forgotten is as good as no dream. Repeat the dream to yourself as soon as you wake up. Better yet, write it down, exactly as you remember it, with all the details. The need to record dreams was already recognized by Daniel (Dan 7:1).

Third, once you remember the dream or see the vision, ask God for help in understanding. Be quiet, listen to God. Ask a prayer group to pray with you. Do not press for the interpretation. Be patient. It may take time to learn to listen to God through symbolic language. The most important prerequisites for listening to God are constant meditation on God's Word and obedience to God in practical matters (Eph 5:1-14).

From Scripture we know that dreams are usually given so that we may understand our inmost thoughts (Dan 2:30). The same is true of many visions. Consequently, visions often prove to be extremely helpful in counseling because they may suggest associations that help the counselee to remember crucial events of the past.

Psychology agrees with this. Freud established that dreams reveal the unconscious. Jung went a step further and taught that our dreams often compensate for imbalance between the conscious and the unconscious. He believed that by paying attention to dream language we can live more balanced lives.

Some dreams and visions, however, are not about ourselves. They are external and may deal with other people or events. The Bible is full of such external dreams and visions. But these are exceptions. The most likely purpose of dreams is to point out problem areas in our own life, to give us guidance or to prepare us for a time of testing. That is why we are most open to them during times of testing or crises:

> For God does speak—now one way, now another—though man may not perceive it. In a dream, in a vision of the night, when deep sleep falls on men as they slumber in their beds, he may speak in their ears and terrify them with warnings, to turn man from wrongdoing and keep him from pride, to preserve his soul from the pit, his life from perishing by the sword. (Job 33:14-18 NIV)

And in Psalm 16:7 we find, "Even at night my heart instructs me" (NIV). Dreams and visions, then, are for instruction. If they are about ourselves, they are like a mirror of the inner self, warts and all. They do not spare us.

Dealing with Symbols

Since we are dealing with picture language, it will be helpful to have some understanding of the symbols used. The most important symbol in dreams is people. They may be our parents, relatives, friends or strangers. Whoever they are, the message is probably not for them, but for the dreamer. They may represent that part of us that is like them. Often there is a shadow figure, or alter ego. It stands for a part of ourselves that we would rather not face.

The birth of a baby may mean the start of a new chapter in our life. Similarly, a death is not likely to be predictive, but represents the dying of some aspect of our behavior, or the end of a phase in our life.

Animals in dreams usually refer to our drives and impulses. I once dreamed about a fourth-floor room where I had boarded while attending university in Rotterdam, Holland. Outside the window of that room, in a large field, I saw some cows. Then I noticed that there were more and more cows, and also pigs. Suddenly I desired to get back to the room, for I perceived the animals were going to attack me. As I hurried towards the room, I wondered why there was now a narrow gate, somewhat broken down. Somehow, I managed to avoid the animals and scramble through the gate. I barricaded it with some pieces of furniture to make sure the animals could not pursue me. I went downstairs, borrowed a bike and rode home, some thirty miles away. For me, this dream was a warning from God about some habits and drives that I should bring under God's control before they got out of hand.

Other symbols are falling, indicating that we are not on solid ground in our life; fighting, usually telling us that we are involved in some inner conflict; the automobile, representing our ego. If we are in the driver's seat, we are trying to be in control, but the wheel may not respond.

John Sandford, a Christian counselor, calls some dreams "state of the union" messages, a report by the Holy Spirit on the condition of our heart and soul. For example, a mild-mannered man may be a violent warrior in his dream. Such a dream may tell him that he has forced his nature out of balance by striving under the law. Repressed urges demand expression. The Holy Spirit does not want us to repress but to surrender, so that we keep the law in the only possible way—by abiding in Jesus Christ.[28]

The Sandfords also warn not to take a message of disaster and doom in a dream as inevitable. There is nothing fatalistic about the Christian faith. God may warn us through such a dream, and call us to repentance or to intercessory prayer. If the warning is heeded, the prediction does not have to take place. Dreams about blessings are not absolute either. If they are not received with faith, they are like a promise that we have failed to realize.[29]

As we pray to understand dream messages, we must also ask God what action to take, if any. About five years ago, I dreamed about a teen-ager in my previous congregation in Toronto. I had heard from friends that he had become part of the counterculture. In the dream, I met with a group of dropouts, all looking the part of prodigal sons. One of them was that teen-ager. I hardly recognized him, with his long, unkempt hair. Love for him flowed into me. Then I started talking with him about Jesus. The most tender and urgent words came from my lips, and I realized that God gave me every one of them. After some time, he started weeping and wanted to become a Christian. The other members of the group had listened intently without saying a word. Now they too wanted to become Christians.

I was sure there was a message for me. But what about the parents of that teen-ager? They were very worried about him at that time. Should I have written to assure them that all would be well? I believe I should have. At the time I did nothing. As it turned out, their son did become a Christian.

The simplest form of a vision is merely to have a person or thought come to mind; prayer is the action required. I once felt a sudden urge to pray for the salvation of some hockey players. One of them was Paul Henderson of the Toronto Maple Leafs. Over a period of months, these players kept coming to my mind for prayer. Then the vision faded. Several years later I met another Christian who that

77

same year had felt the same prayer burden. Then sometime afterward, Henderson and some other athletes testified on a television program that they had become Christians.

Word and Spirit

It is happening! The Holy Spirit is manifesting himself through dreams and visions in abundance as prophesied. What remains is for the church to take notice. The teaching of the church must recognize the vital place of visual prophecy in the ongoing communication of God with his people. The church has ignored the association of outpoured Spirit with dreams and visions, and has chosen to deal with other associations that fit better with traditional theology, such as the outpoured Spirit with illumination of the written Word.

Faithfulness to Scripture as the written Word of God demands an overhaul of the exegesis of Acts 2. A serious treatment of dreams and visions has been left out. Why ignore what the Spirit has expressly put in? Moreover, a theology of the Spirit that leaves out access of the Spirit to our senses is defective from the point of view of Scripture.

The time for such an overhaul is ripe. The Spirit has prompted it. An age-long official silence is being challenged. Thousands of visual prophecies demand a fair hearing. Even the intellectual climate of our day is supportive: modern scientists have pointed out the limitations of the Aristotelian view of knowledge. As a result of this new openness, psychology and medicine, in search of ways to find healing and wholeness, have discovered in dreams and visions "what the Bible knew all along, but Christians had forgotten."[30]

4
Tongues: The Biggest Christian Friendship and Oneness Buster of the Century

George Mallone

Discussions and debates on tongues usually have partisans on both sides—pro and con—who want the help of a one-armed theologian. This authority figure assures us that he will not come to the subject matter with any waffling, no "on the one hand this and on the other hand that." He is expected to pronounce with absolute certainty a position akin to "thus says the Lord." But in fact, those on both sides of the debate need to stop to ask whether the answer is as simple as it is often made out to be.[1]

Let's begin with some basics—a word study. *Glossolalia,* the technical term for speaking in tongues, comes from two Greek words, *glōssa* ("tongue") and *lalein* ("to speak"). Three basic definitions have been given for the word *glōssa*.[2] First, it may refer to the tongue simply as an organ of speech (Lk 16:24). Second, because of a nonliteral translation of 1 Corinthians 12:10, *glōssa* has come to mean, for some, "ecstatic utterances." Along with the New English Bible, at least four other translations have used this term—Barclay, Williams, Goodspeed and Wand. The Greek words *ekstasis* and *existēmi,* from which we get the English "ecstasy," are indeed used in the New Testament. But they are always used of those who observed the phenomena and not those who participated in the phenomena.

This unfortunate translation wrongly associates with *glōssa* the notion of being overwhelmed by emotion and beyond reason or self-control. Although *ekstasis* may refer to a trance (Acts 10:10; 22:17), the primary focus is astonishment and terror which grips an audience which has seen the power and gifts of God (Mk 5:42; Acts 3:10). On the day of Pentecost, when the one hundred and twenty were filled with the Holy Spirit and spoke in tongues, it was the multitudes who were ecstatic, amazed and marveling (Acts 2:7, 12). The one hundred and twenty appeared to be fully in their right mind, but released to praise God.

Thus this unfortunate translation of *glōssa* as "ecstasy" misrepresents not only what happened at Pentecost and at Corinth, but what is happening today. It reinforces studies which suggests that glossolalia is related to schizophrenia and hysteria and that "hypnotizability constitutes the sine qua non of the glossolalic experience."[3] There is plenty of evidence, however, that tongue speakers are not any more or less stable than those who do not speak in tongues.[4]

A third definition of *glossolalia* links it to speaking a language. But what kind of language is it? What is the *new* tongue (Mk 16:17), the *other* tongue (Acts 2:4), the *diverse* tongue (1 Cor 12:10), the *unknown* tongue (1 Cor 14:2) which accompanied the launching of the church at Pentecost? The answer to this question is determined largely by the context in which the phenomenon is described.

Pentecost Tongues
After waiting in obedience to Jesus' words (Acts 1:4-5), the disciples were filled with the Holy Spirit and "began to speak in other tongues" (Acts 2:4). Luke explains the event, saying that there were Jews in Jerusalem who had come

80

from many lands (Acts 2:8-11) to celebrate the Feast of Weeks. Only in Jerusalem could the dispersed Jews celebrate the Holy Convocation (Num 28:26-31).[5] These travelers heard a great noise of praise (Acts 2:11) and made their way to find its source. They described the event as hearing the mighty deeds of God spoken in their own languages (Acts 2:6, 8, 11).

Miraculously the disciples were speaking languages unknown to them, but known and used by dispersed Jews in their various countries. These languages had both form and syntax. The miracle was clearly in the speaking and not in the hearing. The magnitude of the event suggests that it probably will never be repeated, but that does not preclude the possibility that on occasion it has happened in the past and may happen again.[6] Elsewhere in the New Testament, we are not told that the speech miracle of Pentecost was repeated, we are only told that speech activity was recognizable by all as being praise to God. Such an assessment gives us cause to pursue the biblical use of tongues further by reflecting on Paul's correspondence with the Corinthians.

Corinthian Tongues

Paul states that among the gifts of the Holy Spirit there are various kinds of tongues (1 Cor 12:10). Many suggest that the tongues Paul is referring to must be the same variety that occurred at Pentecost. The argument runs like this: Since we have no definition of tongues other than Acts 2, 1 Corinthians and other passages on tongues must be understood in that context. Arguing from this premise and from 1 Corinthians 14:20-25, four conclusions are usually drawn by the most conservative critics. George E. Gardiner lists them:

First, biblical tongues was the supernatural ability to speak in known languages which were not understood by the speaker. It was not babbling or ecstatic speech.

Second, tongues was a special sign for the confirmation of the word for rebellious and unbelieving Israel until the destruction of Jerusalem and the scattering of the nation which began the Time of the Gentiles.

Third, biblical tongues are no longer spoken. The purpose has been fulfilled and the phenomena [sic] has ceased.

Fourth, the Corinthians became fascinated by tongues because their use brought attention to the user. This preoccupation resulted in the misuse of the gift as they edified themselves, disregarding the total spiritual life, and failed as witnesses to their city. The Corinthian catastrophe![7]

It is further argued that tongues speaking today is also akin to this foolish babbling of the Corinthians. Therefore, its source is either demonic or the learned behavior of those who have passively transferred the control of their will to some dominant leader.[8]

A plausible argument, but not convincing, for if we assume that all tongues in the New Testament are foreign languages, then it is impossible to make sense of 1 Corinthians 14. One must candidly ask the following questions of the text in both observation and interpretation. Why would God, in order to have someone speak to him, bestow a foreign language upon that person (1 Cor 14:2)? How do you speak in a foreign language to God in the Spirit and have it as a mystery (v. 2)? How would speaking in a foreign language edify yourself (v. 4)? Is the interpretation of a foreign language something you pray about (v. 13)? How can you pray in a foreign language and your mind not be engaged in the process, to think in form and syntax (v. 14)? Similar questions could be asked of a number of other verses in this section (vv. 16, 18, 27). After comparing the Acts experience and the Corinthian experience of tongues, Oswald Sanders concludes that "since there is such a marked difference between these two manifestations of the gift of tongues, it would not be sound exegesis to build a system of doctrine on the identity of the two occurrences."[9]

These and other problems with the foreign language assumption have led many to the conclusion that in Acts 10 and 19, and certainly in 1 Corinthians 12—14, we have something very different from Acts 2.

At Corinth they were apparently not foreign languages, which Paul denotes by a different word (*phōnē*, xiv.10, 11), because a special gift, not linguistic proficiency, was necessary to understand them; nor were they meaningless ecstatic sounds, though the mind was inactive (verse 14) and the utterances, without interpretation, unintelligible even to the speaker (verse 13), because words (verse 19) and contents (verses 14-17) were recognized, and interpreted tongues were equivalent to prophecy (verse 5). A definite linguistic form is suggested by the Greek words for "to interpret," which, elsewhere in the New Testament, except in Luke xxiv.27, always means "to translate," ... and tongues are probably best regarded as special "languages" not having ordinary human characteristics, inspired by the Holy Spirit for worship, for a sign to unbelievers (xiv.22) and, when interpreted, for the edification of believers.[10]

Perhaps it would be helpful to be a little more exact in describing what tongues is in 1 Corinthians. William Samarin has done fine, comprehensive work on this subject. His definition of glossolalia is more precise than Putnam's, and he concludes that "in spite of superficial similarities, glossolalia is fundamentally not language. All specimens of glossolalia that have ever been studied have produced no features that would even suggest that they reflect some kind of communicative system."[11] Samarin goes on to conclude that glossolalia is some form of extemporaneous pseudo-language.[12]

The pseudolanguage described by Samarin is probably some form of precognitive speech, which is not filtered through the mind for orderly arrangement, and which, when delivered, may sound like language but is really lacking any form, syntax or specific vocabulary. It is not ecstatic, although emotion may or may not be experienced during the speaking of tongues. The mind is functioning, although it is not leading the process. The speaker knows what he or she is doing, but may not know the meaning of what is being said. It is a speech which has been given not only to men but to angels to be used in worship (1 Cor 13:1; 14:2). It is effusive prayer in which the heart and soul are poured out to God.

Let us now see how this definition of tongues fits into the context of Paul's major instruction on tongues in 1 Corinthians 14. Clearly, Paul is rebuking the Corinthian church for its abuse of tongues. But this correction is *not* meant to suppress tongues altogether (v. 39). Equally, there is a preference for prophecy as a clear speech communication from God (v. 1). But again, this is not an argument for suppressing tongues. Having established this much, we may go on to the specific statements Paul makes.

First, tongues speech is directed to God and not to men (v. 2). God is the recipient of the blessing given by the person. The person may have no idea what he or she is saying, but God knows the intention of the heart, and graciously unravels the intercession and praise. Without interpretation, tongues speech is not beneficial for the body.

Second, tongues is speaking mysteries in the Spirit (v. 2). Since the language is precognitive and thus meaningless to all hearers but God, it is a mystery of the Spirit. As C. H. Dodd has said, "An inarticulate aspiration is itself the work of the divine in us, and though we ourselves may not be conscious of its meaning, God knows what it means, and answers the prayer."[13] It is expressing the inexpressible.

Third, speaking in tongues edifies the person (v. 4). As a by-product of praise and intercession, the person is built up and edified in the faith.

Fourth, Paul prefers prophecy to tongues (v. 5). However, to insure that the Corinthians will know of his commitment to tongues he inserts the phrase "Now I want you all to speak in tongues." Not only does this verse state Paul's preference, but it may also give us insight into the Corinthian abuse. It may be a backhanded way of saying that though *all* the Corinthians were speaking in tongues, they should not *all* be doing so because *all* are not gifted to do so (1 Cor 12:30).

Fifth, tongues plus interpretation does edify the entire body (v. 5). The gift of tongues can be used publicly when there is someone to interpret (vv. 6-9, 13, 16-17). The known speech of interpretation is understood by all listeners. They can participate in the message and all add their "amens."

Sixth, when a person prays in the Spirit the mind is unfruitful (v. 14). This verse has been greatly abused and adds fuel to the assumption of emotional instability among tongues speakers. For example, this statement in *Baker's Dictionary of Theology*: "The tongue speaker lost the control of intellectual faculties (vv. 14-15), the tongue being probably a disjointed highly pitched ecstatic series of ejaculations, similar to tongues spoken in times of spiritual awakening experienced intermittently by the church."[14] But it is the presumption of ecstasy and frenzy which leads to the conclusion that there has been a loss of control of intellectual faculties. "Unfruitful" only means that the mind neither produces nor understands the speech. As Larry Christensen says,

When you speak your native tongue or any language

which you have consciously learned, your mind controls what is said. But speaking in tongues is speaking forth prompted not by the mind but the Spirit. The speaker does not decide what sound will come out next; he simply lifts up his voice and the Spirit gives utterance (Acts 2:4).[15]

Seventh, Paul himself admits to being a tongues speaker (v. 18). Attempting to correct the Corinthian abuse, Paul acknowledges that he is thankful to God because he speaks in tongues more than the Corinthians. It follows that he knew what they were experiencing and valued the gift himself. The Corinthian gift was out of control, however, and needed apostolic instruction in order to be used legitimately.

Eighth, tongues is a sign not to believers but to unbelievers (14:21-25). Dispensationalists and other cessationists use this verse as their key to unlocking 1 Corinthians 14. To them tongues must be known foreign languages, by analogy with the unknown language of the Assyrians who had led Israel into captivity (Is 28:11). They conclude that glossolalia is the ability to speak a foreign language and is a specific sign to unbelieving Jews as it was on the day of Pentecost (and in Isaiah's prophecy). The classic pentecostal argument is similar. It holds that people speaking tongues are speaking known foreign languages and that unbelievers will be converted when they see this phenomenon.

By quoting Isaiah 28:11, Paul *is* referring to the foreign languages spoken by the Assyrians. The Assyrian tongues were a sign of judgment on Israel. But the focus of Paul's analogy is the *unintelligibility* and *judgment* of tongues, not tongues as foreign language. He is not trying to identify the Corinthian experience as a foreign language, but as a judgment upon unbelievers who do not (or *will* not) understand.

God had spoken clearly through the prophets to ancient Israel. But when they did not repent, he showed his wrath by breaking off communication with them and sending people of a foreign tongue to rule over them. Clear speech was a sign of God's blessing; unclear speech was a sign of his judgment. So it is with the precognitive language of Corinthian tongue speaking: it was a judgment on those who did not believe, simply because, without interpretation, they could not understand. But clear speech, prophecy or tongues plus interpretation, leads to the conviction and conversion of nonbelievers. Paul pleads with the Corinthians to stop playing with tongues in a childish manner which leads unbelievers to think that they are mad or crazy, and to use them with prophecy in a mature way.

Ninth, tongues for public use needs the complementary gift of interpretation (1 Cor 14:5, 13, 27-28; 12:10). The Greek word *diermēneuō* is used to mean "to translate" (Acts 9:36) and "to explain a meaning" (1 Cor 12:30; 14:5, 13, 27). If Corinth was suffering from unruly polyglotism, then orderly translation was needed. And if it was precognitive speech Paul had in mind, then it would require an equally gifted person to interpret speech which was linguistically incoherent. According to Arnold Bittlinger, that is exactly what is offered in the gift of interpretation:

> Interpretation is a complementary gift which makes possible and meaningful the use of tongues in the meaningful worship. Interpretation is not an accurate translation nor a commentary on the prayer in the Spirit, rather it is a presentation of the essential content in the mother tongue. The one praying in the Spirit is speaking to God, the interpreter receives his interpretation from God.[16]

Paul also makes it clear that there should be no more than two or three tongues and interpretations per meeting (14:27).

Potential Abuses

We have established that it was the abuse of tongues that Paul was attempting to correct. Likewise, there are corrections that need to be heard by those who receive the gift today.

Misinterpreted as Maturity. In some churches speaking in tongues is promoted, explicitly or implicitly, as a sign of Christian maturity. The Scripture maintains, however, that character is the sign of maturity and not our gifts (Gal 5:22-24; 1 Tim 3:1-13; Mt 7:15-23; Tit 1:5-9). We look for character first, then gifts. The perversion of this order has produced many devastating consequences. Some have so spiritualized tongues that it has become a source of great pride, which offends God and also other brothers and sisters in the body who do not possess the gift. Maturity means becoming like the Lord Jesus. To be like him we need refinement. Tongues, when they first appeared at Pentecost, appeared as cloves of fire. That fire symbolized the refining judgment which comes with the Spirit. We must expect that tongues will not any less bring refinement of character today.

Psychological Motivation. A friend told me about a conference he attended where the speaker led the group in collective tongue speech. He told the audience they could each speak in tongues if they simply knew the mechanics. First, they had to open their mouths. Then they needed to loosen up their tongue muscles with certain exercises. After this they needed simply to add a string of lai-lai-lai's to produce the right sound. In the background a particularly emotional piece of music was played on the piano in order to create an environment conducive to "worship."

There *is* an environment which is conducive to discovering the gift of tongues, and the gift can be taught and instructed as one would instruct in counseling or evangelism. With this I have little disagreement. What I object to strongly is suggesting that *all* should speak in tongues and that only in a particular stimulus-response environment does the tongue appear.

A recent survey in the United States suggested that less than half of all people in pentecostal denominations made claim to speak in tongues.[17] Many popular charismatic personalities themselves do not speak in tongues. Kathryn Kuhlman, for example, was never heard to pray in tongues, even by her closest friends.[18] But I seldom attend a pentecostal church where it appears that *any* refrain from this public exercise. Simply explained, it may be that much modern tongue speaking is psychologically induced and not genuinely a gift of the Holy Spirit. I do not blame the individual for this infraction, but the church in general, which for years has ignored the teaching and practice of the gift, so that we now have a difficult time knowing the genuine from the spurious. If the gift does exist, and I believe it does, let us teach and train for it and, at the same time, emphasize that not all possess the gift—because the Spirit does not give it to everyone.

Demonic Motivation. In addition to legitimate glossolalia, there is also false glossolalia which can be demonic in nature. Pagan religions of the first century had ecstatic speech which was frenzied and undisciplined. The cult of Dionysus and the divination of the Delphic Phrygia were known for their tongue speaking.[19] Some of these occult practices may have been brought into the church by new believers. It is also possible that Satan gained a foothold in Corinth by using those who only pretended to have a genuine gift of the Spirit. Their utterances might have been the source of the blasphemous ejaculations, "Jesus accursed," that were upsetting the church (1 Cor 12:3).

Occasionally a church may have to test the tongue of one of its members to secure some understanding of its source. The congregation may be cued to this need by discomfort felt in response to the tongue. The speaker should be asked a number of questions. Has the speaker been involved in any occult practices which have not been repented of and confessed? Was the first contact with tongue speaking in a frenzy or in an environment of stable and controlled emotion? Did the person strive for the gift, or did it come smoothly and naturally? With questions like these we can determine the background of the tongue and conclude if repentance or exorcism of an evil spirit or both might be necessary.

Throughout the entire process there should be love and acceptance of those who have abused this gift. Most of us have perverted our gifts and God has graciously forgiven us. So we need also to forgive those who abuse glossolalia.

Satan wants to convince us that if something is worth doing, it is worth doing wrong. He also loves to employ a strategy of discouragement which says, "You have counterfeited this gift. Now you can never trust yourself again." The church can unwittingly aid and abet the devil if they do not use this encounter for encouragement and growth.

Tongues and Charismatic Theology

Beyond doubt, one of the greatest theological tragedies to befall the church is the suggestion that tongues is a visible sign of having been baptized or filled with the Spirit. This suggestion finds no warrant in Scripture. Tongues did accompany the Spirit's coming at Pentecost (Acts 2:4; 10:46; 19:6). But at other times, when the Spirit was received with equal faith, Luke says nothing about tongue speaking (Acts 2:4-42; 4:4; 6:7; 8:14-36; 9:1-42; 17:32-34). In 1 Corinthians 12:30 Paul clearly inserts the Greek negative *(mē)* to firmly establish that all do *not* possess the gift of tongues. To demand the universality of tongues is to demand something which Scripture does not teach.

Pushing the gift on everyone is not only unbiblical but

can also do great personal damage. "There is no law of tongues in the New Testament," says Tom Smail.

> The legalistic assertion of some Pentecostals that an authentic experience of the baptism in the Spirit must be accompanied by speaking in tongues as its initial evidence, goes beyond any scriptural statement. By the grace of God to speak in tongues is the first new gift of the Spirit conferred on some Christians when they are filled with the Spirit, but this has to do rather with God's gracious response to the need of their personality than the fulfillment of some legal requirement, and the concentration and demand for tongues that results from the imposition of such a requirement leads to most unfortunate pastoral consequences.[20]

I have counseled dozens of men and women who have never possessed the gift of tongues but were forced to manifest it to be accepted by their church leadership. Others did have the gift, but were reluctant to use it because they disagreed with its universal practice and felt that they were only reinforcing this unbiblical thinking. Each of these people was a poor sheep who was manipulated to demonstrate the validity of the Spirit's ministry.

Perhaps we should see in this pastoral manipulation evidence of the genuine desire leaders have to bring their people into the fullness of God's life on earth. Yet Scripture rebukes the rigidity and uniformity which would take God's colorful and rightly arranged body and transpose it into a drab, monochromatic, single-limbed body. Paul's question is still on the mark: "If the whole body were an eye [or a tongue], where would be the hearing?" (1 Cor 12:17).

Although Scripture rejects the "law of tongues," it does not preclude speaking in tongues for *some* when they are filled with the Spirit. As the Spirit rushes into the corners of their lives, awakening new desires for prayer and praise, speaking in tongues will naturally flow forward in some.

Independent of any outside influence, my wife had this experience while interceding for me several years ago. She was released in speech she had never learned before. But as she spoke, she was aware that it was a language which flowed deeply from her own spirit. My experience was quite different. After waiting on the Spirit for several months, I was content that God's filling of my life would be a quiet and gentle work which would not need the gift of tongues. But about five years later, while I continued to seek a fuller expression of personal worship, God gave this gift to me also. It came in such a quiet manner, while I was alone in my office, that it took me over a week to realize what had taken place. I could not attribute it to any "second stage" of blessing or to any filling of the Spirit, for that had occurred quietly and slowly some years earlier. All this underscores the fact that it is the Spirit who sovereignly dispenses the gift as he wills (1 Cor 12:11).

Benefits from Private Use of Tongues

I shall never forget watching a well-known cessationist teacher confronting a university student about tongues. After using the typical arguments for the invalidity of the gift, he implied hopelessness by asking her, "What value does it have?" Her answer was woefully inadequate. Even the convinced need to know the value of the gift of tongues. Listing certain benefits does not necessarily imply that such benefits are unavailable to those who do not have the gift. God will meet the needs of some through tongues. The needs of others he will meet by other avenues.

Personal Edification. In a multitude of ways glossolalia builds up the person (1 Cor 14:4). As one hears words directed by the Holy Spirit passing his or her own lips, there is a sense of God's presence. God is not distant and remote but near and present—within the heart. This often produces a sense of wholeness and integration. The human spirit, submissive to the Spirit of God, is leading the way in the priorities of life. The tongue speaker is not being enslaved by body or by personality in the pursuit of God. In such freedom there is an experience of being in harmony as a spiritual person with a spiritual God.

Tongue speaking also cleanses the mind. Tensions and worries seem to dissipate in the release of the Spirit. There is confidence that we have fully told God of our dilemma and that he has entered into it with us. Relaxation and trust are by-products of a heart that has been poured out before the Lord.

Tongues can also be a help in bearing physical pain. My wife peacefully completed the birth of our second child by singing in tongues throughout the entire labor. This is something which would have been utterly impossible with normal prayer language. Ordinary speech, directed by one's mind is often interrupted and made impossible by pain. But the free speech of tongues can have the same effect of intercession with no mental effort to discern the meaning. God himself knows the meaning of our hearts and responds appropriately.

Spiritual Warfare. It is no secret that Satan is alive and wants to destroy any advance made for the kingdom. Most often his attack is so subtle that it does not reveal its source. In those moments we are oppressed but cannot focus our attention on the source.

Following his description of the armament needed in spiritual warfare, Paul speaks of the necessity of praying "at all times in the Spirit" (Eph 6:18). Charismatics have often erred by making this prayer the exclusive domain of glossolalia. But "praying in the Spirit" may employ words which are understood (to "pray with the mind," 1 Cor 14:15), or words which are not understood (to "pray with the spirit," 1 Cor 14:15). Either is a legitimate description of praying in the Spirit.

In spiritual warfare, the language of the mind can only plead confusion and shed little light. Humbly we confess before God that we do not know the source of the attack or the way out. Praying in tongues is often a means of battle against this vague and elusive enemy. The Spirit knows what is happening in the battle and through tongues is able to lead in the proper intercession.

Once, while on a preaching tour in New Zealand, I was rendered helplessly sick for an entire week. During the confinement I became delirious and hallucinated. I feared for my life and wanted desperately to surrender my ministry and return home. But the Spirit constantly affirmed to me the necessity of fighting the battle with spiritual weapons. Too sick to read or think or move, I could only pray in tongues. Only this seemed to drive back the darkness and despair, replacing them with light and hope. At the end of the week a great victory was won as the ministry resumed in a triumphant manner. Because I had been able to pray through the battle, my spirit was in tune with God to allow him to work through me.

Intercessory Prayer. A woman came to me one day and asked me to pray for her grandson. When I went with her to visit him, I saw an emaciated, blind and almost deaf three-year-old. Only months before, he had been a healthy baby boy. But now in his grandmother's arms he lay helpless, waiting for death. How would you have prayed in that situation? Frankly, I did not know how to pray. But I remembered the teaching of Romans 8:26-28 at that moment: "The Spirit helps us in our weakness; for we do not know how to pray as we ought, but the Spirit himself intercedes for us with sighs too deep for words" (v. 26).

First, prayer is two-party participation. The word *helps* is used only one other place in the New Testament—where Martha beseeches Mary to "help" her (Lk 10:40). This word connotes that some object or chore can only be lifted or done by two people. The Spirit promises to be that other partner when we sense weakness in our prayers.

Second, the Spirit is eager to help us intercede when "we do not know how to pray as we ought." We may know the focus of our prayer, as I did with this child, but we do not know how to pray or specifically what to pray for.

Third, the Spirit is able to take over and pray in and through us. He composes the petitions on our lips. We may be dumb with confusion, but he is able to assess the situation and pray perfectly for it.

Fourth, since it is the Spirit who is praying through us, we can be assured that he is praying according to the will of God: "He who searches the hearts of men knows what is the mind of the Spirit, because the Spirit intercedes for the saints according to the will of God" (v. 27). At that moment we may not understand God's will, but the Spirit has ascertained it and is addressing it back to the Lord Jesus who is seated at the right hand of the Father (Rom 8:34). Praying in tongues is attempting to hitchhike on the prayer Jesus is praying for the person, by listening to the prayer the Spirit is inspiring in our hearts. Through the Spirit we give this concern back to Jesus who intercedes with the Father.

This type of prayer aids the process by which "in everything God works for good" (v. 28). Romans 8:28 is not a catchall verse expressing a philosophy that all is well with the world. It is an expression of confidence that is deeply rooted in the life of prayer. The prayer that is inspired by God the Father, mediated by the Holy Spirit, and prayed back to the Lord Jesus is the prayer that the Father will answer.

As I laid my hands on the little boy's head I began to pray quietly in tongues. I cried out in my spirit, "Lord, I do not know how to pray!" As I continued to pray in tongues, words and thoughts began to come to my mind. As they surfaced, I prayed them in the child's ear. It was neither a liturgical prayer nor a wish-fulfillment prayer. It was a

(handwritten margin note: Can this not also happen in ordinary language? Prayer for guidance in prayer)

prayer designed by God for that specific moment. And only by praying in tongues was I able to pray in the specific direction God desired.

Prayer and Worship. Few of us need to be convinced that our worship language is generally shallow, expressionless and unworthy of our great God. It is essential, then, that in our private worship we begin to cultivate speech which is befitting the majesty, glory, honor and power of God. We need to expand the vocabulary with which we express the intimacy of our relationship with God, finding words which lovers are free to use.

With this foundation, those who have been so gifted can go on to the use of tongues in worship, either spoken or sung. Often we find that our mental vocabulary has been exhausted in worship, and yet there is so much more praise and adoration flowing out of our heart. Inarticulate to the mind, the gift of tongues is clearly a conduit of the heart. It provides the ability to express the inexpressible, to be effusive even when words fail. No doubt such a practice could supplant the necessary mental exercise of meditating on the Lord and striving to speak his praises in known words. But potential abuse need not cause us to fear the use of tongues in speaking to God. Some say tongues is simply mumbo jumbo which bores God. But that conclusion fails to understand that God is more concerned with the nature of our heart and its tenderness towards him than with the vocabulary that we use. And, although most adults do not have this capacity, God, as G. K. Chesterton said, "is strong enough to exult in monotony." We may feel we are boring him to death, but God is big enough not to be bored by our effusive love language.

Receiving and Developing the Gift of Tongues
Wiggling my tongue in my mouth and grunting, hoping that tongues might just appear, I sat in a park, some eight

years prior to receiving the gift of tongues. As I examine my motives for that occasion, I believe my heart was genuinely open to receive all of God's love. I was dry and needy, charred and brittle from professional religious burn-out. Nothing obvious happened that day. But I left the park with the sense that God had heard my desire and that I did not need to beg for this gift. In his own time he would give it, if it so pleased him. Now, after being granted this gift, I think I can point out some helpful principles in receiving and developing tongues.

Reception. The gift of tongues—or any other gift—is not likely to come to anyone who believes these gifts have ceased. It is necessary, therefore, to repent of any theology according to which these gifts have ceased. "Lord, forgive me for rationalizing away your good gifts. Forgive me for quenching and grieving your Spirit. I am open completely to you, Lord. I believe you can give the gifts to me that were a part of the New Testament church."

Acknowledge to God not only that you are open to tongues but that you desire this gift (1 Cor 14:1). Tongues will not bring instant maturity; it will simply be another tool for praise, warfare and intercession. Pentecostals have generally overrated the *desire* for tongues, while evangelicals have underrated it. The desire for tongues is not different from desire for any other gift of the Holy Spirit—the gift of teaching, for example. I was given the gift of teaching because I desired it. Seeing good Bible teachers and the effect they had upon the growth of the body, I began to desire the gift of teaching. I prayed, worked and studied to become a teacher of the Word. If there had been no desire, the gift would not have developed. So it is sometimes with tongues. Cases like my wife's are more abnormal than normal. For most of us this gift will not come when there is no pursuit of it. So step out and boldly ask God for it. Begin to develop your own vocabulary of praise so that worship becomes a part of your life. If you have asked and have begun to praise and worship God and nothing happens, do not worry. "It may," says Simon Tugwell,

> come to you in a prayer a few hours later, or a few days; it may take years. Don't worry and don't turn back; you have made your petition, now stick to it. Do not wonder whether you are going to get it or not, or whether you have been wrong in asking. Continue to pray for it, yearn for it (the Lord may hold it back for a time to increase your desire), until it's yours. The Lord himself will prompt you when the time is right, both for asking and for the receiving. Trust him, and trust relatively the stirrings that you feel in your heart.[21]

Models are also important. For years my image of tongues speaking was of people rolling down church aisles babbling at the top of their voices—an image sufficiently repugnant to take me years to get over. Yet as I met and prayed with a small group of pastors who quietly exercise this gift, I began to see that it was possible to possess this gift with sanity and control. Their experiences did not condition me to speak in tongues. Rather, they modeled for me its proper use and served to smooth out the obstacles in my pathway to receiving the gift.

Although it is not necessary, many people have received the gift of tongues while others prayed and laid hands on them. My wife once prayed with a Christian woman who was longing for this gift. After quietly singing and worshiping with her, my wife placed her hands lightly on this woman's throat and prayed that she would be released. Immediately praise in tongues began to flow from her lips. Others have been released in this gift on their own. As they prayed, it was as though the music of worship had been turned on in their heads. They at once heard melodies welling up in their hearts for songs which had no words. As they opened their mouths, they were filled with the language of praise. For some this release has been highly emotional and quite overwhelming. For others it has been very calm and quieting. But always the Spirit has made an obvious demonstration of his presence.

Development. Once you receive the gift of tongues, you must commit yourself to its development. After the initial encounter, there is often a sense of foolishness and embarrassment over the activity. Often this is Satan's ploy to convince us the gift is not worth having. It is the same type of assault I received after my first sermon: "This is not worth doing. It is not helping anyone."

But as you grow in the gift, you will begin to discern its usefulness. Employ it daily in worship, warfare or intercession. Guard its integrity. Do not let it become "matter of fact business." As we use tongues, it becomes a strong spiritual muscle which aids us in our work for the kingdom. As with the disciplines of Bible study and worship, if we do not practice, we do not grow. But if we develop them, through them we grow into maturity.

Is It for You?

When manipulated or pressured to perform, the natural human reaction is to withdraw. Unfortunately, many have reacted this way to the pressure exerted by proselytizing tongues speakers. But when it is recognized that tongues speaking is neither a pathway to instant maturity nor a uniform guarantee of being filled with the Spirit, and that tongues is a gift for some—but not for everyone, the pressure is eased. So let me ask you a few simple questions.

Would you gladly receive this gift if Jesus wanted to offer it to you? Are you open to the gift of tongues? Do you desire it? If you cannot go this far, can you at least pray that the Lord would make you willing to receive the gift if he had it for you?

Next, although you may not have the gift yourself, are

you willing to allow it to be exercised in your congregation? Using the safeguards of 1 Corinthians 14, are you prepared to respond as a biblical church? In this context, are you prepared to let people grow in their glossolalic gifts? Are you prepared to let them make public mistakes, forgive them, and then allow them to use their gifts again?

Juan Carlos Ortiz is fond of asking Protestants whether they believe first the Bible or the teaching of the church. He suggests that Catholics are more honest because they say they believe the church first. Protestants *say* they believe the Bible, but they are unwilling to practice it. The Bible says that we can dance unto the Lord in worship (Ps 149—150), yet most of us maintain, "We don't dance in our church." Which are we believing first, the church or the Bible?

Scripture also says "Do not forbid speaking in tongues." Yet out of our church tradition we have forbid it. We have maintained the priority of church tradition over Scripture. Scripture tells us that in the body of Christ some members will speak in tongues and that it is an aberration from Christianity if this is not so. From the teaching of Scripture, we would expect the speaking of tongues in biblical congregations. Not to allow it is to grieve and quench God's Holy Spirit. *Though not mentioned in Romans 12, Eph. 4, I Peter 4.*

5
The Recovery of Healing Gifts

Jeff Kirby

I felt numb when my wife and I left the diagnostic hospital. Our eighteen-month-old daughter was diagnosed as profoundly deaf. While sitting with her in a sound-testing booth, noises that pierced and split my head failed to draw the least response from her. Our growing fears and suspicions were finally given a label, however, and in that we were relieved. But now questions filled my mind. Why didn't we realize this before? What would it be like to raise a deaf child? What would her life be like as an adult? How does this relate to God's will? Where have all the miracles gone? Many of these initial questions, though still unanswered, are now formulated better. Jessica's deafness motivated me to inquire of the Bible, relevant theology and history concerning the place of healing today.

A nagging question for me, even prior to this diagnosis of deafness, was the way the Bible seemed to promise more than it actually delivered. "The prayer of faith will save the sick" (Jas 5:15). "He who believes in me will also do the works that I do; and greater works than these will he do" (Jn 14:12). How was one to interpret these verses when clearly no one, at least in my suburban evangelical environment, believed or expected such things? Early on, I had a hunch that more had been lost to humanistic enlightenment, dispensationalism, liberal or existential theology, and fear of the loony fringe than we guessed. Pragmatically, Jesus was correct when he said, "It is not those who are well who need a physician." Christians should not be afraid of divine healing, but should seek rather for a pastoral theology of hope and faith in a redeemed community of love.

Simply speaking, the "gifts of healing" (1 Cor 12:8-10) concern the restoration of health to the physically afflicted. The Greek plural, *gifts* of healing, suggests great variety in those equipped with healing gifts and in the effects rendered by them. The grace gift of healing is a tangible parable of the spiritual purpose of all charismata—the strengthening and upbuilding of the body. The working of miracles overlaps healing but covers a much wider range of mighty deeds. Jesus and the apostles, for example, raised the dead, cast out demons and performed miracles upon nature. Luke records: "And God did extraordinary miracles by the hands of Paul" (Acts 19:11). This chapter will focus primarily on healing, examining the role of healing in the Old and New Testaments as well as on the recovery of a healing ministry today.

Healing and Salvation in the Old Testament

In the beginning God surveyed his creation with delight. Plush vegetation and foliage, beast and bird, dry land and sea—he rejoiced in them all. God saw all he had made and declared it to be very good. And this included humans: the extension of his own identity, made in his own image, the apple of his eye, the crown of his creation. God's heart broke the day his masterpiece was ruined by sin. The damning effect left humans spiritually dead, psychologically fragmented and physically diseased. The environment too was cursed, left groaning for a day of restoration. God promised to act (Gen 3:15).

Salvation is the activity of God directed to those who suffer and are in need of his help. His salvation is illustrated by the preservation of Noah and his family from drowning, floating safely in the ark above the torrents of judgment. God led the enslaved Israelites out of Egypt as a father would scoop up and carry his little boy in his arms (Hos 11:1-4). Upon their deliverance from the tyranny of Pharaoh, God made a promise: "If you will diligently hearken to the voice of the LORD your God, and do that which is right in his eyes, and give heed to his commandments and keep all his statutes, I will put none of the diseases upon you which I put on the Egyptians; for I am the LORD, your healer" (Ex 15:26). Karl Barth has called this verse "the divine Magna Carta in the matter of health and all related questions."[1]

This preventive prescription related the whole lifestyle to physical health. This ancient promise established what is now being recognized within holistic and whole-person medicine, namely, that health is intricately related to the moral, psychological and spiritual well-being of a person. An indispensable dimension of the human personality is the need for a meaningful life principle or purpose. A healthy person is one who participates in significant interpersonal human relations, productive work, and creative rest and recreation. Being included in the redemptive history of God gives one the necessary purposefulness to life.

Unfortunately, Christian theology has often reduced healing to a mere sign which may accompany salvation. But this schism between healing and salvation makes healing the unnecessary extra and salvation the essential. Healing should be viewed, instead, within the context of God's continuing activity of blessing rooted in creation. As D. C. Westermann has written:

> Blessing is a continuous action, it does not consist of iso-
> lated outstanding events or moments, it operates through-
> out human life from conception—the basic meaning of
> blessing is fertility—through birth, growth and maturity.
> Blessing is effective in the development of a person, in
> the unfolding of his physical and mental gifts, it lies in
> every challenge and achievement, in work and its fruits.
> Peace, the wholeness of the community, belongs to bless-
> ing; to be physically whole, to flourish, to succeed, neces-
> sitates a "whole" community.[2]

Obedience to the revealed law of God was to insure the
physical and spiritual well-being of the people of God. "I
am the LORD, your healer" (Ex 15:26).

In the Hebrew covenant community, all healing, whether
by the instantaneous intervention of a man of God, a home-
spun remedy, or nature's own time, was understood as the
work of God. In the Hebraic mind, *salvation and healing were
synonymous concepts,* parallel modes of divine activity.

Elijah restored the life of the son of his hostess by repeated prayer (1 Kings 17:17-22). Elisha raised from the
dead the child he had prophesied would be born (2 Kings
4:18-37). Naaman, the commander of the Syrian army was
cleansed of his leprosy by the testimony of a Hebrew slave
girl and the repeated washings prescribed by Elisha (2
Kings 5).

When King Hezekiah lay dying, Isaiah the prophet made
a house call and bestowed the news, "Thus says the Lord,
'Set your house in order; for you shall die, you shall not
recover' " (2 Kings 20:1). The king wept bitter tears of re-
morse and despair. And he prayed. Meanwhile, Isaiah was
receiving a different message from the Lord: "Turn back,
and say to Hezekiah the prince of my people, Thus says
the LORD, the God of David your father: I have heard your
prayer, I have seen your tears; behold, I will heal you. . . .
And I will add fifteen years to your life" (2 Kings 20:5-6).

Also to the prophet Isaiah was given insight into the redemptive ministry of God's Son. Seven hundred years before Christ, Isaiah uttered an amazing word:

Surely he has borne our griefs
    and carried our sorrows;
yet we esteemed him stricken,
    smitten by God, and afflicted.
But he was wounded for our transgressions,
    he was bruised for our iniquities;
upon him was the chastisement that made us whole,
    and with his stripes we are healed. (Is 53:4-5)

Christ's mediatorial dying for sin is intimately related to disease. "There is little question but that physical healing is placed under the sign of the cross. It is an integral part of the redemption process," wrote Charles Farah.

> It is very clear that healing and the Atonement are bound together. If healing is not in this passage, neither can we count on anything else. . . . As Christ took our sins upon Him and acted as mediator between us and the Father, so He took our sickness upon Him in a substitutionary way. This does not mean merely a symbol, but in our stead and in our place, and He not only took them away, but bore them for us.[3]

The commentator Delitzsch concurs: the "mediatorial sense remains the same."[4]

This does not mean (as many Christians think) that all believers are already healed if only they would claim it. A family I know repeated Isaiah 53:4-5 over their dying father, unwilling to hospitalize him, sincerely convinced that at the last moment his cancer would vanish. It did not, however, and their subsequent guilt and self-condemnation has healed only slowly.

The application of these verses seems both mysterious and complex. There have been many theological spats over whether healing is in the atonement. To me, the issue is not whether healing is in the atonement, but at what point healing is realized. All of God's gracious, saving gifts come to us because of Christ's sacrifice. But *when,* in the course of God's redemptive program, these gifts will be ours to be claimed and appropriated remains unclear. Does healing take place now or later? On earth or in heaven? Certainly the reign of God over disease and death will one day be complete (Rev 21:3-4). His reign will be only partial until he comes in glory. Living creatively with this tension between the "already" and the "not yet" is one of the more challenging dimensions of our discipleship.

The psalmist too spoke of healing and salvation as two sides of the rescue operation of God. Healing is one dimension of being saved.

Bless the LORD, O my soul,
    and forget not all his benefits,
who forgives all your iniquity,
    who heals all your diseases,
who redeems your life from the Pit,
    who crowns you with steadfast love and mercy,
who satisfies you with good as long as you live
    so that your youth is renewed like the eagle's.
    (Ps 103:2-6)

The Old Testament lays the foundation for our understanding of healing. Our need for healing is due to our rebellion from God's creative purpose. God has graciously initiated salvation to recover and restore lost humanity. Healing in the Old Testament is an aspect of God's saving activity. Although at times miraculously instantaneous, it is more often a process much like growth which leads to wholeness *and* holiness within the wholesome community.

The Healing Ministry of Jesus
Over the dusty hills they poured, hundreds of Mexican-

Aztec Indians, carrying their sick children and their dying parents. They brought those with broken limbs which had never been properly set, blind ones whose sunken eyes were without pigment, children with hands and faces dried and swollen, the infectious, and the near dead. Word had traveled quickly that our team of voluntary doctors, dentists and Christian workers had come for two weeks of ministry and service. Nearly four thousand people were treated in those days. Many had been substantially helped. All knew that it was God's love that had motivated Christian people to come great distances at their own expense to help others. Was it similar to this on the dusty hills of Palestine nearly two thousand years ago, when God's own Son of righteousness arose with healing in his wings?

Jesus Christ of Nazareth is unequivocally the most celebrated and successful healer of human malady in history. The proportion of the Gospels devoted to the healing ministry of Jesus is striking. According to Morton Kelsey, "Nearly one-fifth of the entire Gospels is devoted to Jesus' healing and the discussions occasioned by it. . . . Forty-one distinct instances of physical and mental healing are recorded in the four Gospels, but this by no means represents the total. Many of these references summarize the healings of large numbers of persons."[5]

The fact that Jesus healed many of physical, emotional and spiritual disease is a pillar of evangelical faith. John's Gospel concludes with these words: "But there are also many other things which Jesus did; were every one of them to be written, I suppose that the world itself could not contain the books that would be written" (Jn 21:25).

Healing and the Kingdom of God. The healing ministry of Jesus demonstrated that the anticipated kingdom of God had come. Centuries before, Isaiah had prophesied that Messiah's ministry would include the healing of the blind, the deaf and the lame (Is 35:5-6). Jesus alluded to this passage when sending assurance to John the Baptist that indeed the messianic ministry was under way. The relationship of Jesus' healing ministry and the kingdom of God is a consistent theme in the Gospels.

In Matthew 12:22-29 Jesus responded to his critics' ludicrous suggestion that he was actually empowered by Satan. His exorcisms were tangible evidence, he replied, that the kingdom of God had come. Jesus had entered the strong man's (Satan's) house (this evil age) and was making spoil of his goods. In Mark's Gospel the deliverance of demon-oppressed people caused the crowds to inquire by what authority he ordered evil spirits to flee (Mk 1:27).

Luke's Gospel records the preaching mission of seventy disciples. Their assignment links the announcement of the kingdom of God with healing: "Heal the sick . . . and say to them, 'The kingdom of God has come near to you' " (10:9). Jesus informed the disciples, upon their triumphant return, that while they exercised their ministry he had witnessed the tumbling down of Satan's power (10:18). Essentially, the kingdom of God means the reign of God and the triumph of God over his enemies. Demons, sickness and death itself must yield to the greater authority and power of the kingdom of God.

Jesus' healings confirmed his messianic claims, but were neither undeniable proofs nor mere shows of power. His works caused the crowds to reflect, in words reminiscent of Genesis 1:31, that Jesus had "done all things well" (Mk 7:37). To those who had no faith, however, witnessing Jesus' miracles led only to bewilderment and hostility. Jesus rejected the Pharisees' craving for miraculous side shows (Mt 16:1). On the other hand, Jesus appealed to his audience to accept his divine identity on the basis of his miracles (Jn 10:38; 14:11). He did not reject faith which was affirmed by signs. He did, however, rebuke faith which was based solely on signs and wonders (Jn 4:48). The miracles of Jesus were not spectacles, they were powerful evidences that the age of salvation was beginning to be fulfilled.

The Tender Compassion of Jesus. Jesus also healed for another—some would argue a *greater*—reason. His immense love and compassion compelled him to heal. Mark 1:41 is representative of many verses that reveal Jesus' motive for healing: "Moved with pity, he stretched out his hand and touched him, and said to him [a leper], 'I will; be clean.'" In Matthew 12:12 Jesus defends his healing miracle of restoring a withered hand by appealing to the immeasurable worth of the individual before God.

The compassionate disposition of Jesus reflected in full the attitude of the Father towards human suffering and illness. God is often faulted for creating a world full of suffering and evil. The issue is complex both philosophically and theologically. But surely it is inappropriate to blame God for a problem he did not initiate and, in fact, one which he has sought to alleviate at great cost to himself. God sent his Son to inaugurate the kingdom and "destroy him who has the power of death, that is, the devil" (Heb 2:14). God is not the cause of suffering and sickness; he is its cure! Jesus' ministry and death guarantee this.

If Jesus saw himself as the Messiah, then he represented the essential nature of God himself and was his specific messenger, and his healings therefore sprang from the essential nature of God. . . . Jesus laid the attitude of God toward sickness out on the counter where all could see it.[6]

The Healing Ministry of the Apostles

It was nearing the three o'clock public prayer service in the Jerusalem temple. Peter and John, still observing the pattern of Jewish worship, were making their way through the crowds when their eyes riveted upon a lame beggar stretched out on the steps before the Beautiful Gate. Those marvelous temple gates, plated with silver and set in gold, were the backdrop for the apostles' public healing debut. "I have no silver and gold, but I give you what I have; in the name of Jesus Christ of Nazareth, walk," exclaimed Peter (Acts 3:6).

In that instant a surge of healing power regenerated those shriveled limbs long atrophied because unused. The lame man entered the temple with Peter and John "walking and leaping and praising God" (Acts 3:8).

Peter and John were simply continuing what Jesus had begun. Luke opens the Acts of the Apostles by saying that in his Gospel he had recounted that which "Jesus began to do and teach." The obvious implication is that Acts records what Jesus *continued* to do through the apostles by the power of the Holy Spirit. The ministry of Jesus was not to be a fading memory but an ongoing reality. The beachhead of the kingdom of God that Jesus had made was to be expanded through the apostles.

Jesus commissioned the Twelve and then the seventy to preach and to heal (Lk 9:1-2; 10:1, 9). The apostles healed paralysis, demonic possession, fever, dysentery and blindness. Twice people were raised from the dead. Individuals and large groups were healed.

These signs and wonders were demonstrations of apostolic authenticity. Paul reminds his readers that his ministry was accompanied by signs, wonders and a demonstration (*apodeixis*) of Spirit and power (1 Cor 2:4). This Greek word *apodeixis* is a technical term for proof drawn from observable facts as opposed to theoretical reasoning. Paul's concern was that Christian faith should "not rest in the wisdom of men but in the power of God" (1 Cor 2:5). Just as Jesus was attested by God "with mighty works and wonders and signs which God did through him" (Acts 2:22), so God bore witness through the apostles "by signs and wonders and various miracles and by gifts of the Holy Spirit distributed according to his own will" (Heb 2:4).

While we must be wary of the dangers of jumping to irresponsible conclusions on the basis of what the apostles did, we can at least draw some preliminary deductions. First, Jesus himself participated in a ministry of healing which fulfilled ancient prophecies. His healing miracles were evidence that the kingdom of God, the tangible reign of God, had begun to invade history. Further, Jesus called and empowered his followers, both apostles and nonapostles, with the continuation of his mission. This mandate and the nature of the kingdom are evidently still normative. Finally, miracles of healing served the dual purpose of authenticating the divine source of the gospel and the genuineness of its messengers.

Where Have All the Healings Gone?
Given that Jesus' healing ministry was continued by the apostles, what were the factors which led to the decline and disappearance of healing abilities *after* the apostles? Were only the apostles endowed with gifts of healing? That healing ceased with the apostles is a notion that is commonly held and seldom questioned. We feel safe knowing that our faith began with such supernatural flair, and even safer knowing that nothing similar will happen in our churches this Sunday. But what is the evidence?

Many beyond the apostolic band possessed healing abilities. The commissioning of the seventy to preach and to heal was a foreshadowing of the church's ministry. In Acts, Peter, John, Paul, Barnabas, Steven, Philip the Deacon, and a "certain disciple named Ananias," all performed miraculous healings. Clearly, some possessed this charisma of healing at Corinth. The Galatian Christians knew the reality of ongoing miracles, to which Paul appealed as evidence of God's grace active in their midst (3:5). The letter of James makes clear that faithful prayer and anointing with oil were expected to facilitate healing (5:14).

111

The patristic literature of the church's first three centuries supplies substantial evidence that miracles did not end with the apostles. Justin Martyr, writing in the middle of the second century, spoke of the reception of gifts of healing and mentions Christians who were healing in the name of Jesus. In his work *Against Heresies,* Irenaeus distinguishes true Christian teachers from false counterparts by their ability to perform works of healing. Specific cures mentioned include: giving sight to the blind; giving hearing to the deaf; curing the weak, the lame, the paralytic; and the frequent raising of the dead. Furthermore, Irenaeus establishes the attestation of these works before watchful pagans, and notes that even unbelievers were healed, which often led to their conversion.

Augustine, whose theological genius dominated the West for a thousand years, disparaged healing in his early days. Later, in his epic *City of God,* he spoke of how he changed

once I realized how many miracles were occurring in our own day and which were so like the miracles of old and also how wrong it would be to allow the memory of these marvels of divine power to perish from among our people. It is only two years ago that the keeping of records was begun here in Hippo, and already, at this writing, we have nearly seventy attested miracles.[7]

Evelyn Frost, in her classic contribution *Christian Healing,* lists over a dozen factors which led to the decline of the church's healing powers.[8] At the conversion of Constantine, for example, the church's public identity changed and a floodgate was opened to secularization. Faith was exchanged for the growing power of human intellect expressed politically and scientifically over the environment.

An early schism between faith and science has hampered both fields ever since. Religion was perceived as the enemy of scientific progress. The growth of knowledge gave rise to specialization, making the doctors responsible for the body and the clergy for the soul.

Theological aberrations developed which neutralized at the outset any chance of healing faith. The physical body was increasingly viewed as inherently evil and unworthy of divine visitation. Sickness was interpreted not as an enemy of the kingdom of God but rather an agency of God's discipline and intentional will. The promise of physical healing in James 5 was reinterpreted as spiritual healing which became the basis of extreme unction or last rites. A wonderful promise of God to aid in Christians' health became a mere ritual at their death.

The absence of healing power became a focal point around which certain theological systems were formed. Calvin and Luther agreed that healing gifts had been withdrawn by God in order to give preeminence to the preached Word. Much later, dispensationalists argued that God's purpose for miracles had been accomplished, and demythologizers concluded that these events had never happened.

Sometimes, however, a theological system is not adequate when confronted with human need. Philipp Melanchthon, Luther's co-reformer, had become seriously ill in 1540. Melanchthon was bedridden and his death was imminent. Upon visiting him, Luther knelt and prayed for his recovery. He wrote on the wall the words of Psalm 118:17, "I shall not die, but I shall live, and recount the deeds of the LORD." Instantly Melanchthon's condition visibly improved. This healing miracle Luther always considered one of the greatest he had ever witnessed.[9]

Restoring the Healing Ministry

While writing this book, the authors together went on a retreat to a nearby Catholic abbey. During one of our meals with the monks, we sat by a young novitiate named Michael. He told us a very interesting story about himself. Until June

1976, Michael had been a successful disc jockey in Montreal. On the twenty-sixth of that month, doctors diagnosed symptoms that had recently appeared as Hodgkin's disease. They told him he had perhaps a week to live. In that hospital Michael surrendered himself utterly into the hands of God. "I completely abandoned myself to God's providence and care," he said glowingly. "I did not demand a healing from God; I only asked that our dear Lord's will would be done. That was one-thousand-seven-hundred-and-fifty-five days ago, and I thank him for every moment that he has given me." Since then Michael has lived in a kibbutz by the Sea of Galilee and joined a Benedictine community.

As this robust man walked away from us, I wondered how many thousands of Michaels, and praying mothers with sick children, praying children with sick mothers, have been secretly tucked away in the memory and heart of God. These are not the events of systematic theology, church history textbooks or doctoral dissertations. But they are the events of life that belong to people who relate to the living God.

The current resurgence of interest in the healing ministry has not always found an adequate theological environment within which to grow. But now some scholars are integrating responsible exegesis and openness to the gifts of the Spirit. Theological renewal alone, however, is not enough. Clark Pinnock has written helpfully on this question in a recent issue of *Christianity Today:*

> It is not a new doctrine we lack. What we need is a new dynamism that will make all of the old evangelical convictions operational. We need not so much to be educated as to be vitalized. It is not a doctrine of the Spirit that we need, but a movement of the Spirit, pervading and filling us, setting our convictions on fire.[10]

The movement of the Spirit is in God's hands. But we can prepare ourselves for it in a number of ways.

Study the Word. Leaders and laity alike should turn afresh to the Scripture. Bible study is often reduced to brief devotional spurts because of hectic lifestyles. Yet we all know that there is no substitute for consistent, thoughtful, Bible study.

I recently led a workshop for our church members on developing skills in inductive Bible study. Part of the seminar was given to individual study and reflection. Afterward some of the participants confessed that although they had spent several years in the church, this was one of their first experiences in serious Bible study.

Richard Foster wrote sharply to this need in *Celebration of Discipline:*

Many Christians remain in bondage to fears and anxieties simply because they do not avail themselves of the discipline of study. They may be faithful in church attendance and earnest in fulfilling their religious duties and still they are not changed. They may sing with gusto, pray in the Spirit, live as obediently as they know, even receive divine visions and revelations; and yet the tenor of their lives remains unchanged. Why? Because they have never taken up one of the central ways God uses to change us: study.[11]

A good starting point for study would be a soaking in the Gospels. We may discover that the subjective portrait of Jesus our minds have painted is in sharp contrast to the historic Jesus of God's Word. The Acts of the Apostles portrays a young church enamored with its Lord and doing the works that he had done. The epistles place the healing ministry in an orderly context among the many workings of the Spirit. As we inquire of those passages relevant to healing, we must seek understanding that goes beyond our cultural and rationalistic prejudices.

Read other Literature. Walking into a Christian bookstore today should be preceded with the prayer "Lead me not into temptation." The avalanche of intriguing and helpful new books is a wonderful resource—and a potential danger —to Christians of the Western world. Christian healing has been the topic of many studies, some powerfully beneficial and others weak or misleading. We must discern the wheat from the chaff among the secondary literature on spiritual gifts, and in particular on healing gifts.

One of the more informative and responsible works on healing I have read is Morton Kelsey's *Healing and Christianity: In Ancient Thought and Modern Times* (Harper and Row). It is "an attempt to provide a theological foundation, based on historical and scientific understanding, for a serious ministry of healing today."[12] Thoroughly and logically, from historical and biblical material, Kelsey builds a platform for religious healing in the modern world. He provides a philosophical framework which makes divine healing utterly acceptable and suggests practical steps for healing in the church today. This is an essential book for anyone interested in the healing ministry.

A recent publication by Ray Lawrence, *Christian Healing Rediscovered* (InterVarsity Press), is a simple and humble introduction to the subject. This Anglican vicar writes sensitively of his experiences and places them within a theological framework. This is the book to start with for those who are reading on the subject for the first time. Its format is appropriate for house-fellowship groups or Sunday-school classes.

Francis MacNutt's two books, *Healing* and *Power to Heal* (Ave Maria Press), come out of the Catholic charismatic renewal. *Power to Heal,* written three years later than *Healing,* integrates positive, faith-building insights with a discussion of suffering and death. Both books are challenging and have been widely read.

J. Sidlow Baxter has written *Divine Healing of the Body* (Zondervan). Here is a careful treatment of the healing ministry as practiced historically and as taught popularly today. Baxter concludes with a radiant and intimate testimony of his wife's healing of terminal cancer. Baxter himself was later healed of diabetes, after having a vision in his hospital bed of an illuminated text from Psalm 103 promising renewed health and strength. This book I recommend to those who question or distrust things "charismatic."

One final recommendation is Charles Farah's *From the Pinnacle of the Temple* (Logos). Farah blends responsible, biblical insight and balanced faith. This book is especially helpful in its critique of the popular "faith theology." Those who have been snared in the notion that healing depends exclusively on one's faith need this corrective. Farah establishes the place of the sovereignty of God and the element of mystery in a healing theology. He also grapples with the question of when believing faith becomes presumptuous faith.

You may also discover to your delight that your own denomination or church affiliation has undertaken helpful studies in the area of healing. I was delighted, for example, to read "The Relation of Christian Faith to Health" adopted by the one-hundred-seventy-second General Assembly of the United Presbyterian Church.

Exposure to Healing Gifts. In addition to study of Scripture and secondary literature, we should acquaint ourselves with those whom God has gifted in this ministry. It may come as a surprise that many intelligent and responsible Christians are exploring the healing ministry. Find out who in your geographic area is experimenting and seeking to grow in a ministry of healing. You may even meet brothers and sisters in Christ from churches that up to now you thought were spiritually suspicious. That in itself could be a marvelous healing. I have attended meetings and seminars conducted by pentecostals, Catholic charismatics and inner-healing evangelicals. Some of the presentations I have had to reject totally, while others have been quietly disturbing, prodding me to a greater faith in God's healing work.

In addition, I participate in a biweekly, interchurch fellowship for pastors in my city. We meet regularly for study, sharing and especially intercessory prayer. We recently held a morning seminar on healing which fifty pastors and their wives attended. We spent time in Bible study, discussion, questioning and prayer. This led to a further evening seminar designed to train our elders and lay leaders. This helpful and foundational learning experience has moved our churches forward in a healing ministry.

Begin to Pray. We must also begin to pray about this dimension of God's truth. Paul exhorts us to "earnestly desire the spiritual gifts" (1 Cor 14:1). Ask God for the full expression of spiritual gifts in your life and community. If you are in leadership, you have a responsibility to communicate the whole counsel of God and his work in healing. Perhaps you could begin by setting up an inquiry group within your church that could study, read, share and pray together. In time, this group could begin to invite people to visit who need healing prayer.

The New Testament clearly links prayer and bodily healing. "The prayer offered in faith will make the sick person well; the Lord will raise him up" (Jas 5:15 NIV). There are many important factors concerning healing which reach beyond the scope of this chapter. Anointing with oil, while believed to have been medicinal in some cases, now must be viewed sacramentally. What restores the sick one to physical health is not oil but the prayer offered with it.

The effect of intercessory prayer is great if the one praying is righteous and does so in faith. James cites Elijah as an example of the dynamic results which can occur when a person beseeches the living God. If by prayer Elijah could hold back or send the rains, then surely the united prayer of the church can call down God's healing power.

Our pastors' fellowship has heard numerous stories of elders and house groups gathering to pray for the sick. God has graciously healed several of cancer, tumors and other internal disorders as well as various aches and pains.

Steve, a young businessman who had been following Christ for a number of years, awoke one morning to find large lumps under his chin and armpits. Consulting his doctor that day, he was immediately hospitalized. Two Christians in the hospital, one a physician and the other a biophysicist specializing in cancer research, took a look at their friend's biopsy report. "A textbook case of Hodgkin's disease!" reported one of them. Within a few hours, word spread to Steve's house group and church. The entire community launched a prolonged session of prayer and fasting. The house group maintained a twenty-four-hour prayer chain. Every visitor took time to lay hands on Steve and ask God for his gracious intervention. There was no sense that we had to demand Steve's healing or even encourage him to more faith. We simply trusted God and beseeched him for mercy. Graciously, God answered our prayers. Three days after Steve entered the hospital, the lumps disappeared. He had received no medical treatment. Remission, wrong diagnosis, miracle? Who can say? All that can be affirmed is that God hears and answers prayers. All situations may not end this way, but Scripture instructs us that all who are sick should at least be prayed for in this way.

Of Those Not Healed
Matt was a fine high-school athlete. On one of the first plays from scrimmage, Matt thrust himself at an approaching fullback. There was a snap, followed by the immediate loss of all physical sensation. Matt the linebacker became Matt the quadriplegic. Many people visited Matt over the ensuing months and prayed for his healing. One even prostrated himself before his bed and claimed he would not move until

Matt was healed. Eventually he walked out again, but Matt did not. In spite of the misdirected zeal of many Christians, Matt's faith and courage grew.

Those of us who enjoy life in relative health can place an unbearable burden on those who suffer. Our prayers for healing can have a threatening and condemning effect unless we offer them with humility, love and support. Job's verbose and theologically misguided friends kindled God's wrath because they had not been right in what they had said about God (Job 42:7).

With our practice of the healing ministry, we must build a parallel theology of suffering, not as a place to hide when healing does not come, but as a way of understanding another mode of the work of God in the lives of his people —suffering. "For it has been granted to you that for the sake of Christ you should not only believe in him but also suffer for his sake" (Phil 1:29).

Jesus Christ delivered and healed people victoriously. He also suffered for them vicariously. He has become to us the wounded healer, and our own lives will no doubt be a reflection of his, both wounded and healed.

6
Equipping for Spiritual Gifts
Paul Stevens

The first time I heard someone say, "It takes a mature man to rejoice in his wife's achievements," I was sure it applied to someone else—not me. But it *did* apply to me. Gail, my wife, was the first in our family to become involved in neighborhood evangelistic Bible studies. That was the first achievement.

Then she took the plunge into an inner-healing ministry. At first, though supportive, I was cautious. But I was soon reassured and excited about yet another of her achievements. And I began to experience joy, for while coming to terms with my wife's spiritual discoveries, I not only witnessed God's work in people's lives, but I was able to reformulate some important principles for helping people grow and develop in the use of spiritual gifts. These principles involve *exposure* to gifts, *experimentation* with gifts and then *extension* of the gifts in full-orbed maturity and training.

Together these principles spell equipping for ministry, and that is what this chapter is all about. The idea that we might have a training program for prophecy or some other neglected spiritual gift seems ludicrous, if not offensive. On the other hand, I am forced to ask, if we have a training program to equip teachers, why should it be incredible to think of training for healing or prophecy? If all the gifts are from God, surely equipping must concern all the gifts.

Paul says, "Prepare [equip] God's people for works of service, so that the body of Christ may be built up" (Eph 4:12 NIV). "Prepare" or "equip" (RSV) translates *katartismos,* which is, among other things, a medical word employed by the Greek physician Galen for the reduction of dislocations and fractures. Equipping the saints includes this idea of bringing into proper connection various members of the body of Christ. The verb which has the same root, *katartizō,* means "to mend" as fishermen will clean, mend and store nets to make them ready for proper use. Paul uses this word in Galatians 6:1 for restoring a brother or sister who has fallen. Both these words suggest that equipping is not merely informing or supplying needed skills but correcting improper and unfruitful relationships. The primary meaning of equipment is to make complete and ready for service through training and discipline.

If this chapter seems at points more corrective than directive, it is because in the matter of neglected spiritual gifts the body is "out of joint." Limbs and members with these gifts gather together in special groups or even separate churches which are usually known for the exaltation of tongues or healing. Sometimes two or three who have one of these specific gifts meet together in small huddles of illumined spirituality within a local church, but apart from the rest of the body. Fear or pride could be the reason. These dislocated members need to be equipped, put into place, as do the rest of the members.

Jesus himself was involved in an equipping ministry. It is quite remarkable that, after a successful and fruitful public ministry of preaching and healing, he deliberately turned to a training ministry of the Twelve. Indeed it seems that he answered his own prayer request in Matthew 9:38, "ask the Lord of the harvest . . . to send out workers into his harvest field," when "he called his twelve disciples to him" (Mt 10:1 NIV). Paul's ministry with Barnabas, Silas, Timothy, Aquila and Priscilla is similarly impressive and will be considered later.

What fully convinces me of the sure, biblical foundation for an equipping ministry is what Acts and the letters of Paul tell us about life and ministry in the local church. There we see the local churches fully endowed by God with the gifts needed for ministry in the church and the world. The fullness of God has been given to the body of Christ (Eph 1:23). God has supplied apostles, prophets, evangelists, as well as pastors and teachers "to prepare [equip] God's people for works of service" (Eph 4:12 NIV). Though we should benefit from all that God is doing through parachurch training agencies, my settled conviction is that it is in the local church that the neglected spiritual gifts encouraged by this book should be discovered and developed.

Now let's examine the principles of equipping for gifts— exposure, experimentation and extension.

Equipping by Exposure

"She'll come back speaking in tongues, you can be sure." I had mixed feelings when a friend said that about Gail. She had been invited to a women's conference out of town and the diet was frankly "charismatic." Saturday night she returned. In the middle of the soccer game I was playing, I called out to her, "Well, did you?" She had not. But something beautiful had happened that cracked open my thinking in the whole area of ministry development. Actually, an accident had occurred, a leadership accident.

Somehow, Gail got drawn into the planning of the weekend. Even more important, since the weekend was directed towards prayer, she got to pray with the leaders for needy and hurting people. These were inner-healing prayers, prayers to appropriate God's forgiveness, prayers for the release and the filling of the Spirit, prayers for healing in the emotional lives of women. No one seemed to realize that she was not a "charismatic," as popularly defined. Gail came home convinced, however, that God had called her to explore and to engage in this inner-healing ministry.

Exposure to Something More. What happened that weekend I am calling exposure. It plays an essential role in opening people to what God wants to do in their own lives—both in ministering to them and supplying them with gifts—and in opening them to what he wants to do in the lives of others in the body. Frequently, we simply do not move beyond a safe, comfortable gift ministry because we have never seen or heard anything more. God's first ministry to us is to shatter our preconceptions and break down the walls of our prejudices. Too many people and too many church leaders fail to appropriate God's full blessing for the church because they have never witnessed a healthy expression of particular spiritual gifts. Seeing people healed and praying alongside more experienced women convinced Gail that the gift was being used biblically and that it was desperately needed in the church. But I too needed the same exposure.

Partly to make a personal assessment of what my wife was now embracing, I went with her to St. Luke's Episcopal Church in Seattle for a seminar on inner healing. No one knew that I was there as a "snoopervisor." The problem was that the conference was designed to *involve* people in the experience and snoopervisors were not welcome. Within a couple of hours, I was dealing with my own, very particular needs for inner healing. As a result of some incidents in my past, with which I had never dealt properly, I was dependent in an unhealthy way on the praise and approval of others. The desire to be accepted and approved stemmed from some unresolved hurts, which God began to heal that day.

But he not only began to heal my personality that week, he began to heal my methodology. I could not be an adequate trainer of people if I was fearful of the gifts God wanted to give to his people. And for me, exposure was one way of relieving the fear.

Why is it relatively easy to train teachers in the church and hard to train healers? Surely, one reason must be the repeated exposure given to the ministry of teaching. In the practical priorities of the local church, teaching is deemed the one thing needful. But God says otherwise (1 Cor 12:21). Exposure to less common spiritual gifts, or to any neglected ministries, is crucial to our expectations. In order to think that God might wish to do something more than *we* have already experienced, we usually must see and hear him doing that through someone else.

Exposure Outside Your Bailiwick. Conferences are one way of gaining exposure to new people, new scriptural understanding, and participating in the kingdom of God in new ways. Books serve this purpose also. Books on neglected ministries allow the concentrated experience of another to expand our own vision and faith. Inter-church gatherings, such as take place in my own city, allow us to participate in dimensions of worship and fellowship that challenge our present securities.

I found myself at one inter-church communion service praying for twenty or thirty people. This one wanted to be filled with the Spirit. That one needed healing. Fifteen or twenty of us were serving people in this way. During this experience those of us serving as well as those on "the other side of the communion rail" were exposed to something beyond our safe and familiar Sunday morning routine. We were all "out of our depth," depending on God in a new way.

Traveling to other cities to see what God is doing in other churches and experimental works is another means of exposure. I once traveled to Boulder, Colorado, to see what God was doing in a work where the gift of helps had been developed and exalted to its proper dignity and value. Why should I not also travel to a church where God has poured out his Spirit in prophecy? Without such exposure our spiritual expectations may shrivel and settle into a mechanical repetition of the kind of ministry that "has always been."

Exposure Where We Are. Though inter-church exposure can create new openness, what is even more crucial is learning to revive these neglected spiritual gifts and new ministries without leaving our local church. How can we build into the lives of our churches the capacity for continually discovering "something more for God"? If we fail to address this matter, we shall only perpetuate the common syndrome of getting "fired up" at a conference only to be "doused to death" when we get home.

The truth is that God gives all the gifts he wants in the local church. We may not have every gift (assuming we could make such a definitive list), but no spiritual gift should be lacking from the full complement God wills for a particular local body. How could a gift be lacking if Christ is fully present to accomplish his work? Our task, then, is to discover the gifts God has given, to bring them out of hiding, to honor them as God's loving provision, to domesticate them. In a word, our task is to equip for them.

Teaching about the gifts will help. Deliberately modeling some ministries is the next step. It is also important to research the desires and abilities that God has given the members of the body. House groups are ideal for asking, How do you want to express your worship to God? Have you ever spoken in another tongue, a tongue of worship and praise? When you pray for sick people do you find that God gives you faith to believe in their healing? What dreams have you had which have been significantly true or important? Through a curriculum which we have developed for use in the house groups of our fellowship, we develop gift lists of all the members by affirming one another's ministry. The list is never definitive or final, but it helps people see the diversity of God's endowments.

Exposure through Life-on-Life Training. What could be more ludicrous than a one-man-band ministry? How well I remember wilting as I sat through ordination sermons which exhorted fledgling ministers to be everything: prophet, pastor, teacher, evangelist, healer, administrator. The idea that *one* person in the church can be the "minister" and everyone else "members" is one of the most dangerous heresies practiced today. The story of its institutionalization and widespread acceptance is a sad one indeed.

In contrast, what characterizes biblical church practice is communal, not solitary performance. Again and again Paul tells the believers in Ephesus that they are "together," "fellow citizens" (2:19), "joined together" (2:21), "being built together" (2:22), "heirs together" (3:6), "members together" (3:6), and "sharers together" (3:6). In light of these "togethers," we are left with the conclusion that we will never develop gifts alone.

The essence of ministry development in the local church is life intersecting with life. That's where God speaks grace and power. What better way is there to experience God's grace and power than to deliberately team up with someone with a different gift? Find the person most unlike you in the church and do something with that person. Visit the sick or teach a class or plan an event together. Expose yourself to some of the "craziest" people in the fellowship. They have something unique to offer you. One wonders what Paul meant when he said: "If we are beside ourselves, it is for God" (2 Cor 5:13). Have you heard someone sing in the Spirit? Ask to pray and worship with him or her.

The Paul-Timothy relationship—a hand-picked younger disciple—is appealing. In my opinion, however, it is not offered in the Scriptures as a universal training model. Contrary to expectation, Paul implies that we will not always be receiving God's nurture from a more mature, older brother or sister. We may be discipled by the weakest member of the body for "the weaker are indispensable" (1 Cor 12:22).

Frequently, attention is focused on the influence of Paul on Aquila and Priscilla, who served with Paul in at least two cities and accompanied him on some travels. Their seminary training was simply that relationship. So effectively did Paul expose them and train them that Aquila and Priscilla were able to disciple others. With great skill they took the outstanding preacher Apollos aside to expose him to something more (Acts 18:26).

But surely it is not wrong to ask (though Scripture does not fully answer) what influence Aquila and Priscilla had on Paul, or, for that matter, what influence Luke the Physician had on Paul. What better place to be exposed to God's next step than right where we are—and through those who are weaker members, as well as through the strong? "Never allow the thought—'I am of no use where I am'—because you certainly can be of no use where you are not."[1]

Exposure through Expressed Needs within the Church. Sandra was in our house group that met weekly. She always sat awkwardly on a chair because, as we all knew, she had a back problem. A recent pregnancy only exacerbated the problem. Without any explanation, she did not come one week. The next week she did come but with stress lines on her face that indicated more than physical pain. Almost as a ritual we asked, "Are there any prayer requests tonight?" Sandra was bold enough to be vulnerable: "I would like you to pray for my healing. I have become aware that my back problem is not merely physical but related to the way I handle stress." Her decision called us to decision. We could not ignore her if we loved her. Yet none of us had the gift of healing. We resolved to pray for her healing despite our unspoken fear that nothing might happen and Sandra would be worse off.

We did pray, fitfully and half-believing. And as we prayed something happened that no human could orchestrate, something which reinforces the idea that spiritual gifts are not endowments given for Christians to *possess* but manifestations of the will of the Spirit. One in our group was given a special sensitivity to Sandra's need and prayed into her heart. It seemed appropriate to lay hands on her. One in particular in our little group of learners found himself functioning not merely from general loving interest: He had a specific interest in healing which had never come fully to light in the group until that night. God was with us and a substantial measure of healing did take place in the following days. Sandra's need exposed the gift. Her vulnerability and our response to her need exposed us all to a further dimension of ministry among us. It also revealed a second crucial principle in equipping for spiritual gifts: *experimentation.*

Equipping by Experimentation
Douglas Hyde's remarkable book *Dedication and Leadership* chronicles the afterthoughts of a former communist, now a Catholic Christian. He writes: "The majority of people who join the Communist Party do so knowing very little about communism. This is as true of the intellectuals as of the workers. The potential recruit *sees the Party in action.*"[2] He goes on to detail at what point the candidate is trained. "The instruction of the new Party member does not normally begin immediately after he joins. Quite deliberately, and with good reason, the Party sends its new members,

whenever possible, into some form of public activity *before instruction begins.*[3]

This Communist training principle could have been borrowed from Jesus of Nazareth! Jesus told Peter and the others to follow him *in order to become* fishers of men. His "come and see" invitation was soon followed by "go and tell." Jesus sent them out by twos, by twelves, by seventies. He sent them out long before they were ready—at least by our standards. Those men and women who turned the world upside down hardly knew the content of the Apostle's Creed. They saw Jesus in action and were involved in service long before their instruction was complete.

It is hard to imagine a church system more unproductive for equipping ministries than the one normally promoted. If by brilliant and creative human ingenuity a church structure were devised to *prevent* the development of gifts, it could hardly improve on what we have. Large groups of people assemble to hear one person or a very few exercise their gifts, while the majority ruminate, evaluate or otherwise passively listen. Seldom are people trusted with any concrete ministry until they have proved themselves as Christians for several years. Little or nothing is expected of new Christians except that they study, listen and watch until they have grown mature. A high priority is placed on cognitive learning. Errors in doctrine or simple doctrinal immaturity are regarded as sufficient reason for people to do nothing except listen. Has an *enemy* designed this church structure?

Jesus' training methods are in contrast to common church training today. Until perhaps two-and-a-half years of active service had passed, Peter appeared not to know that Jesus was the Christ, the Son of the living God (Mt 16:16). We have reason to think he had healed people and cast out demons long before he could adequately express in words his belief about Jesus. The unsuccessful attempt of the disciples to heal a convulsive child (Lk 9:40) suggests that they were experimenting *beyond* their faith and spirituality, not safely within it.

We should strive to create an atmosphere within a church in which spiritual gifts could be *tried out by anyone.* Even as I write this, I shrink a little because it sounds blatantly antispiritual, if not antisupernatural. But I ask myself this question: How did I develop the gift of teaching God manifests through me from time to time? By having the freedom to experiment with teaching. What then is needed for healthy experimentation?

1. An Experimental Climate. Shortly after becoming a Christian, I was asked to give my testimony at a young people's meeting. I led what in those days was called a devotional. As time went on people created situations in which I could minister to the body long before I dreamed that God had given me the gift of teaching. What might have happened if opportunity for experimentation had not been given? And I now wonder whether certain spiritual gifts may never have surfaced within me because I have never had an opportunity *to try.*

Clearly, Scripture suggests more than one way of discovering spiritual gifts. Timothy, for example, received gifts *by the laying on of hands and prophetic utterance* (1 Tim 4:14). Prophecy thus serves and edifies from time to time by suggesting what ministry may be given an individual by God. The influence of such suggestive prophecy on the ability of a person is almost impossible to overestimate. It is also necessary to say that prophecy which stems from carnal manipulation can be destructive to the real gifting of a person.

2. Awareness of Our Own Spiritual Desires. A crucial condition for experimentation is a healthy attitude toward motives. Often it is assumed in Christian groups that what *we* want to do is surely the exact opposite of what God wants us to do. But how can this *normally* be if we are "new creatures in Christ" and have "the mind of Christ"? Therefore, reflective prayer and meditation on the way God has made each of us and the desires he has generated within us since our conversion are vital first steps. Certainly, not all our motivation is from God. But if Christ lives in us and if the old has passed away (2 Cor 5:12), *what we want to do for Christ will usually be an indication of a potential gift.*

We should expect that gifts will commonly be discovered in the fellowship through a combination of redeemed motivation and experimentation. Each of us is a fraction of Christ's body. Each has some special way of blessing the body. It is like our God to lead us to do this by making us *want* that very ministry. That is why, in our house groups, it is wise to ask from time to time, "What do you like to do in the area of Christian service?"

3. A Climate of Expectation. "Nothing new will happen" is often a self-fulfilling prophecy. One component of faith is expectancy. Those of us who suffer from the "little faith" disease need to be constantly asking: Is there something new God would do among us? Am I prepared to be surprised by God? Is there some ministry of the Spirit in this situation which I am frankly not open to receiving or giving? Without desiring personal glory, am I open to being an instrument for praising God and loving his people through *any* of the spiritual gifts, and with *all* the fruits of the Spirit?

4. Responsibility for Correction. The responsibility of shielding the church from the potential dangers of experimentation lies with the plural leadership of elders. If someone ministers in an unedifying way, it is the task of the leaders to deal with this. This shelter of loving correction frees both the congregation and the experimenting believer from the inhibiting feeling that "if it goes wrong, the church will be destroyed." Plural leadership is essential to this shepherding role, since not every elder, nor any one pastor, has discernment concerning all gifts of ministry.

In our own fellowship I am able to make eye contact with different elders and house leaders in response to somewhat questionable situations. And I know that I can count on some brothers or sisters to be discerning when others might be unaware of all the dimensions of a certain ministry.

5. Willingness to Try. One of my first steps in the area of prophecy was responding to a mental picture I was given while praying for a young woman. During a communion service, she had confessed at the altar rail her utter spiritual dryness and her desire to be refreshed in the Spirit. I prayed for her for a minute or two, and then God put in my mind a scene of rain falling on a desert. At first the sand was so dry that the falling rain had little noticeable effect. Only a slight dampness was apparent. But as the downpour continued, it became evident that the land was being refreshed. Soon small rivulets and streams formed. Finally the streams became a river that fanned out to reach other dry areas of the desert.

Should I share this vision with my sister? I thought. What if it was not a prophecy but just a creation of my own mind? (Can these two be totally and finally separated?) I had never prophesied formally. I decided to risk telling her what was in my spirit, knowing that this visual prophecy was in harmony with the great promises of Scripture. She received it as a message of encouragement from God. And that tender first experience encouraged *me* too. For not many weeks later I was able to share a similar prophecy-vision with the congregation, knowing that I was free to fail and free to share a word of encouragement even if it did not prove to be specially anointed.

6. House-Group Structures. The small group is a splendid structure for equipping for gifts. The idea of the "church in your house" needs little defense, since it is so thoroughly rooted in Scripture (Rom 16:3-5; 1 Cor 16:19; Philem 2; Acts 2:43-47). In *The Problem of Wineskins,* Howard Snyder summarizes the advantages of the small group structure: "Its smallness and intimacy allow a high degree of communion and intercommunication. It does not require formal structuring; it can maintain order without stifling the informality and openness conducive to the freedom of the Spirit."[4] Many churches are finding that, in our society, the rhythm and balance of "sanctuary church" and "house church" is required to realize the full potential of New Testament Christianity.

Here is a quiverful of ideas on how to discover gifts in small groups:

☐ Minimize the emphasis on gifts and maximize the emphasis on ministry. Instead of trying to discover "the healer" in your group, pray as a group for healing. Allow God to show who may be especially gifted in healing. Focus on the Lord and people's needs.

☐ Get everyone in the house group involved. There is something for each person to do. One of our house groups, cleverly, assigns a wide variety of tasks to people: writing absent members, phoning people about prayer needs, arranging a common meal and visiting the sick.

☐ Practice gift affirmation. At least once every year a whole evening should be spent in this exercise. Each person in turn should be affirmed by as many members of the group as possible. Rather than insisting on a strict gift designation, "I think you have the gift of . . . ," a better way is to affirm the ministry, "God ministers to me through you by. . ."

☐ Emphasize the things everyone can do. Everyone can share a Scripture. Everyone can pray. Everyone can encourage or help. By emphasizing the ministry of practical love, we leave the door wide open for God to show each person his or her unique place in the fellowship.

☐ Find out what every member *wants* to do. Have an evening when everyone shares dreams of what they would like to be and do if options were unlimited. Important clues about ourselves and others will certainly surface.

☐ Try some new things in this small group which might be premature in the "sanctuary church." Free singing to a common Christian praise song can be explored by a small group of worshiping believers who are comfortable enough with each other to experiment.

☐ Do not neglect worship as the central focus of the group. Without worship most groups gravitate to mere Bible discussion or sharing, whereby important dimensions of a God-centered ministry are missed. Singing praises, speaking out our love to God, and breaking bread together open the door wide for spiritual gifts.

7. *Participatory Worship Services.* Corporate worship must be restructured (or de-structured) to allow people to be surprised by God. Idols, whether physical or mental, never surprise because "they have mouths, but do not speak" (Ps 115:5). Those who worship such fixed and static conceptions of God become "like them" (115:8), rigid, stereotyped worshipers. Surely, one of the marks of the personhood of God is his ability to surprise. But what room is there for surprise in the traditional worship service? With the order of service laid out, there is sometimes little room for God.

On the other hand, the totally unstructured service, without order or visible leadership can easily gravitate to the unacknowledged liturgy of habitual religion. As Peter Gillquist says: "There is nothing more distasteful during a public worship service than having three or four people scattered throughout a room doing 'something unique' to worship the Lord and embarrassing everyone else to tears."[5] What is needed is a worship context that has sufficient order to draw the many private expressions of worship into a unity, but sufficient freedom to invite spontane-

ous participation. Paul's corrective word in Corinthians
(1 Cor 14:27) assumes this balance.

The fellowship I serve uses a thematic approach to worship.[6] Within this context there are pauses and long silences
during which the worship leader invites participation.
Often a leading suggestion can both encourage people and
bring a certain unity and order. "The characteristic I appreciate about the Lord this morning is . . ." At certain periods
an invitation is given for people to share a word from Scripture or to bring a word of exhortation to the fellowship.
Specific designations like "miraculous gifts" or "special
gifts" are avoided in order to encourage people to share
what they have, even if they are uncertain whether it falls
into the category of a spiritual gift.

Three or four times a year the Lord's Supper is celebrated differently from our weekly practice. Teams of people, sometimes seven or eight couples, stand behind the
specially arranged long table. As people come forward in-
dividually to receive the elements they are asked if they
have any specific need for prayer. In response to the incredible diversity of need, gifts of healing and prophecy
are sometimes expressed. By involving nonelders in this
praying ministry, a whole new group of people in the fellowship are exposed to the kind of prayer ministries usually
experienced only by elders (Jas 5:13).

8. Organic Mission Projects. The standard approach to
community outreach is this: survey the community with the
best sociological tools, ascertain the most pressing needs,
hire staff to facilitate the program and hope that you can
get some volunteers to help. Nothing could be more alien
to the New Testament. There the Spirit directed, restrained
and empowered. Sometimes, Paul was prevented by the
Spirit from going to a needy place because God had other
plans. It is quite apparent that Paul had a long-range plan
for his mission, which was to establish a self-propagating

Christian church in every major center of the Roman Empire. But the month-by-month implementation was a matter of much spontaneity and Spirit direction. It depended on the provision of concrete individuals—like Lydia (Acts 16:14), Titus (2 Cor 7:6), Aquila and Priscilla (Acts 18:3)—to take up the mission.

If Jesus is the head, then surely he can direct his body into mission. One of the clearest indications of his leadership is his provision of gifts and visions. A recognition of the particular gifts and particular visions he has given the members of a local church must be part of discovering his agenda for mission. Thus, by discerning his body we can anticipate his power and provision for what he wants us to do.

Garth had a vision for day camping as a summer ministry in the community. This was not a project in the minds of the elders, but, as it turned out, it was in the mind of the Lord. Because the elders know that vision is not limited to themselves, our fellowship has established a mission-development fund in its annual budget to facilitate the vision of any member. This concept of mission arising from visions and dreams within the hearts of members maximizes the scope for discovering gifts.

Equipping through Extension

Focusing on some of the more spectacular gifts, as we have in this book, has certain dangers. One is that we might be heard to say these gifts are more important than other gifts. No such hierarchy exists in the New Testament. A second danger is that the manifestation of gifts in our lives may be deemed to be more important than character development. Sanctification and the development of mature Christian character is the preoccupation of New Testament writers and the worthy subject of numerous books. Perhaps the most strategic danger in stressing gifts is that if all the gifts are operative in our fellowship, we might be deluded into thinking there is nothing more—we have arrived. This is a major reason why extending the equipping process is the third matter that needs to be explored.

My thesis is that the full development of gifts like prophecy, tongues and healing requires that they be intimately joined to and complemented by the entire range of ministries of the local church. How, for instance, could a ministry of prophecy become fully developed without an extensive grasp of the whole counsel of God in the Scriptures? Dreams can be useful in counseling, but unless the recognition of dreams is wedded to a growing skill in listening and praying with troubled people, we could easily be faulted for naive superstition. My wife, Gail, finds that inner healing needs to be coupled with counseling and has prepared herself through a variety of courses and supplemental experiences to be equipped in that way.

What frustrates ministry development today, in my view, is that hardly anyone believes it can happen at the local church level. The local church, it seems, has too many agendas to give itself to a serious training enterprise. With rampant professionalism and the expertise mentality dominant in today's church, how can First Baptist Church in Pumpkin Center ever hope to offer a credible alternative to Bible school or seminary? The practical universality of the clergy-laity distinction means that "tentmakers," those who engage in serious ministry but support themselves (Acts 18:3), will always be second-class citizens. Furthermore, the casual attitude we take to local church life and any training enterprise within it militates against serious extension of the gift ministry. There are no fees, no examinations, little structure, no diplomas and no recognition.

But turn the argument around. If equipping for gifts is difficult inside the local church, is it possible outside? While thankfully recognizing the influence and contribution of seminaries, training centers and Bible schools, to which I myself owe too much to be cynical, let me offer a few critical assessments.

An institution set apart is generally unrelated to the normal life of the Christian. Normally, the Christian works, relates to family and friends, witnesses, and engages in a wide variety of relationships and ministries, all in connection with involvement in an imperfect local church. Training centers lack this holistic emphasis. Academic training and achievement leads some people to accept more responsibility in local churches than they should. Too frequently, two or three years in a training center creates a false impression of maturity and the conviction that professional Christian service is the best way to serve God. And this happens without the continual testing and proving of the Spirit by a local church. Paul advised Timothy to appoint elders and deacons who had already proved themselves in life (1 Tim 3:1-12). Generally, one or two gifts, usually teaching, counseling or evangelism, are overly emphasized by a parachurch training agency. That is their strength; it is also their weakness.

I think it is not overstating the case to say that there is no better place to gain complete training for ministry than in the local church. Did Paul have anything else in mind when he desired to "present every man mature in Christ" (Col 1:28)? And could there be any better place to see some of the most neglected gifts come to maturity than in the ongoing life of the local assembly?

What the local church has to offer is the potential of a fully scriptural context for developing ministry: shared worship, shared life, shared mission. Multiple and plural leadership models are found there. Some of the best learning comes, Paul would say, from the weakest brother. Always, in the local church, there is the opportunity to learn humility and practical love through voluntary service and by performing unspectacular serving tasks. A short manifesto for extending the equipping process could be summarized in two phrases: train the involved and involve the trained.

Train the Involved. Everyone who is doing anything in the church should be helped to do it better. We have already seen how the communists, unconsciously modeling the training method of Jesus, get people involved immediately. Then they train them. One can hardly imagine a more strategic group to receive this kind of in-service training than small group leaders. They are already involved and have desire, motivation and a clear task. They are like pastors of little flocks. Why not create a training program for them which, in the course of two or three years, will give them as much help as possible in ministering to their little flocks?

Worship leaders also have a strategic role to play in the ongoing life of the church. Why should they not be led into biblical and historical study of worship? Better still, why should they not worship together under the leadership of a more experienced worship leader who can lead them further?

Some churches have an extensive adult education program. Our own fellowship has developed an integrated curriculum for congregational life. We all agree to study a book of the Bible over a period of about ten weeks. A study guide is prepared by members of the fellowship. Personal study questions are a part of each week's study, and a group study on the same passage is offered. Finally, the Sunday teaching ministry brings to a climax the individual and small group study of that week. Instead of getting Acts on Tuesday at house group, Leviticus in our quiet time and Christian social action on Sunday, the body shares a common and cumulative learning experience.

Do people get bored with the same text all week? Not once have I heard someone say this in over eight years of experience. And this type of learning is within the range of even the smallest church. Even more important, in some ways, than the value of an indigenous training and learning program is the value of producing it. Involving various members in researching, writing, testing and applying is in itself a learning and training opportunity.

If someone clearly manifests the gift of evangelism, pour some energy into maturing that gift. When someone evidences a potential in prophecy, begin to develop that ministry with a good reading program. Guided exposure to other situations and ministries where this gift has found full expression would also strengthen this gift.

Someone who evidences a healing ministry will be highly motivated to make the most of it. A sensitive equipper can guide that person to resources and to others who are more mature in that ministry. Recently I was able to take one of our elders to a seminar on praying for the sick. It is no accident that this elder was one who had recently prayed with me for someone's healing and has evidenced a particular concern for this ministry.

Everyone doing anything should get help to do it better. And, according to the apostle Paul, the people called to help them are the leaders (Eph 4:11-12). This is the role of the trained, paid pastor. In the fourth chapter of Ephesians, Paul says that God gave apostles, prophets, evangelists, pastors and teachers "to prepare God's people for works of service." That is, *the function of the leading minister is to make himself dispensable.* This is precisely what the average clergyman does not do and what the average congregation is trained not to expect. Ministers, pastoral leaders, should strive to lead their flocks to the place where they are dispensable to the ministries of the church *except as equippers.* What a revolution in leadership this concept would incite!

Involving the Trained. Everyone who is getting training

should be involved. The idea of learning without application, doctrine without doing, is anathema to the whole Scripture. Larry Richards, among recent writers in practical theology, has thoroughly criticized the school concept of training.[7] For good reasons, he sees the normal approach to training as too cognitive, too heady, too abstract. What we need is something better.

The something better will not develop without a great deal of experimentation. Failures may exceed successes. But this writer is committed, and has been for almost twenty years, to developing within the local church a facility for fully training its members. Surely, some courses are needed. It ought to be possible, for example, for all to gain an adequate grasp of the Old and New Testament through guided study. They do not need a university degree to do this. Nor should they have to submit to an essentially academic program. A survey course in the Scriptures, if properly conceived, can lead participants to systematically read through the whole Bible to learn not only the major themes but how God leads us to action and obedience through his Word. Again, I am not saying there is no need for seminaries; I would not want to see the equipping done exclusively by the local church. But for too long the local church has been overlooked and neglected as the principal location for equipping God's people.

Seminars on evangelism, counseling, inner healing and true spirituality can be developed which aim to ensure the marriage of information and application. Adults in particular learn best when their own experiences become a major ingredient of the learning process. Those studying prophecy might spend a weekend together where a wide diversity of gifts may be manifested. Such seminars will not only cultivate existing gifts, they will also uncover new gifts in the body. New recruits will be found for vital ministries in the local church and God's people—all of them—

will find and exercise their special service to the body.

God needs no help in developing the gifts we have studied. He is sovereign. In great wisdom, *he* has distributed gifts in the body. *He* plants motivation in our heart to love him and serve each other through gift ministries. He is at work in us, and we labor, struggling with all *his* energy (Col 1:29). God doesn't need any help. But we do, which is the reason he gave gifts designed to equip the body. In great wisdom, too, he designed the local church to encompass both common life and leadership training.

Our rigid structures, minimal expectations, habitual religion and shriveled spirituality are like the stone in front of Lazarus's grave. Only Jesus could bring him to life with his word. But the friends of Lazarus *could* help bring their friend to life—they could roll the stone away. That's equipping—putting the members in joint, moving the stones away.

7
From Fear
to Faith
George Mallone

My wife and I recently met four people who were given the gift of tongues over ten years ago. We met them at a conference on church renewal and national revival. The conference included one session on personal spiritual renewal but little emphasis on spiritual gifts, especially tongues, prophecy and healing. Through private counsel and prayer with several individuals, my wife and I "smoked out" these four people. We also learned, to our sorrow, that their home churches and friends were so hostile to this gift that they had shelved it for all these years. It was occasionally used privately, but that was all.

Each of them was a mature Christian, dedicated to the Lord, to personal Bible study and prayer, to sharing the gospel and living out the ethics of Jesus. And they were all afraid—afraid to exercise this gift.

This chapter is intended as therapy for those who cannot exercise controversial gifts because of fear. It is to be prayed through as well as read through. You need to come to grips with whether or not fear is governing your life, to discern the source of any fear, and to be released from it to exercise the gifts God has given.

It takes very little psychological insight to see the sources of most of our fears. We seem to be paralyzed by what others think of us and expect from us. We are also hindered by self-doubt and misgivings about ourselves because we cannot trust ourselves to exercise gifts properly. Another problem, even for the most devoted Christian, is often a faulty view of God which causes us to fear him in the wrong way. Let us see what the Bible has to say about these three sources of fear.

Fear of Others

The Bible has over thirty Hebrew and Greek words for the common human emotion of fear. Some fear is positive and necessary, but some kinds of fear are unwarranted. Scripture admonishes us to respect (fear) and submit to the legitimate claims of government (Rom 13:1-3) and employers (1 Pet 2:18). But the Scripture does not enjoin or permit us to be slavishly intimidated. "The fear of man lays a snare, but he who trusts in the LORD is safe" (Prov 29:25). Fear of others is a trap. Once caged, we have no freedom. Our daily diet is fed by fear, and our exercise or lack of it is prescribed by fear. Incarcerated, our spiritual muscles weaken.

In 1976, my fellow elders provided for me a one-month leave of absence for spiritual refreshment and restoration of vision. I suspected that new vigor would come from meeting exciting new people and hearing of various effective programs. The vigor God had in store for me, however, came from a different source. I had only just unpacked my bags and had my first quiet time, when God began to speak to me about fear of my fellow elders.

This was my first pastorate. The church tradition was foreign to my experience, but not to my sympathies. Graciously, the elders tutored me in the way of that heritage.

From time to time, inevitably, there arose disagreements about how the past, both in Scripture and in tradition, was to be brought into the present. At such times I found myself backing down from my own convictions. Several of the men were my own age and an unhealthy competition began to develop with them. I feared their leadership gifts and felt that if they were given more recognition, there would be no place for me.

After several days of prayer and meditation, it became clear to me that I had begun to treat my own brothers as enemies. With my elders in mind, I began to read the deliverance psalms of David—Psalm 56:1-2, for example. Fear of these men had led me to view them as my adversaries. Repenting of such a notion, I was then led by the Lord to a further conclusion: even if from time to time these men did appear to be my enemies, I did not need to fear what they could do to me (Ps 56:3-4). I was to trust in the Lord for my reputation, ministry and sense of fulfillment. With these convictions firmly established by the Lord, fear of others began to disappear. Upon resuming my duties as an elder, I was able both to be stronger in my convictions and to be more willing to submit to each of the other elders. The elimination of fear produced unity, not an individualistic brashness which knew no submission.

Fear of Ourselves
If it is not fear of others that is an obstacle to manifesting spiritual gifts, it is often fear of self. This timidity stems from the conclusion that we are inadequate and useless. "God couldn't use me! I would blow it for sure! I remember one time when I thought God told me to do something and I did it. Boy, did I make a mess of things. I can't trust myself after that incident." A sense of worthlessness, a distrust of one's own motives, and a hesitancy in Christian

experience are the result of fear.

Paul's word to the youthful Timothy is a good corrective here. "God did not give us a spirit of timidity but a spirit of power and love and self-control" (2 Tim 1:7). The cowardly reluctance we feel about using our gift is not from God. He is not pleased and people are not blessed by such a posture. The Spirit given by God is one of power. The Greek root for *power* means the ability to do something. By the Spirit, God enables us to overcome our natural timidity.

God's Spirit is also the spirit of love. By this love, I do not value myself higher than I ought, nor lower than an estimation given by God (Rom 12:3). I can contribute my gift to the body not because I am so great, but because God has in love deemed me a worthy child, fit for ministry.

It is also a spirit of discipline which causes us to walk in a sober, self-controlled manner. Our minds, disciplined by the Spirit, have no time for self-condemning and despairing thoughts.

Romans 8:15-16 highlights the same point. "You did not receive the spirit of slavery to fall back into fear, but you have received the spirit of sonship. When we cry, 'Abba! Father!' it is the Spirit himself bearing witness with our spirit that we are children of God." We need no longer fear ourselves because God has chosen to adopt us as his children. He has given us free access to him, the opportunity to intimately greet him as our daddy. Fear of self is dispelled by God's love. When we cry out to him, "Abba! Father!" the Spirit immediately takes those words and bears witness to us, "Yes, you are a child of God. Access and ministry are yours."

Fear of God

Scripture everywhere affirms that the proper attitude of a creature to the Creator is fear in the form of reverence and awe (Job 28:28; Ps 111:10; Prov 14:26-27; Jer 32:40). But there is another fear of God cultivated by some Christians that is both unhealthy and unbiblical. God is thought of as overly demanding. Jesus told a parable of a nobleman who gave one pound to each of ten slaves—an advance of nearly one hundred days' wages (Lk 19:11-27). Each of the slaves was to do business with the money until the nobleman returned. When he returned, an accounting of the stewardship was made. One servant made ten pounds, another five. A third slave, fearing the exacting nature of the nobleman, hid his money in a handkerchief and had not increased the pound investment. For this, he lost everything. A wrong perspective of his master left the slave unable to function. We likewise, fearing that God would never be pleased with less than a perfect development of our gifts, hide them.

Like the fearful slave, I have often felt that God was exacting too much from me. The cost of using the gifts was too much. There was always a misunderstanding of the gifts and the need for more biblical definitions. I have wondered if it was even worth the effort. But as the parable points out, God does not exact overmuch from his stewards. The percentage of investment increase, the result from using a gift, is in God's hands. But the using of the gift is our responsibility, and we are not free not to use them. Only a healthy attitude about the Lord who distributes gifts can enable us to use those gifts confidently and profitably. The gifts are given not to overwhelm us nor to lead us into temptation. They are given graciously by a God who trusts us with his resources.

Overcoming Fear
In each chapter we have attempted to disarm unwarranted and unbiblical fears about using gifts. But that does not mean we have carte blanche on the use of these gifts. Each

149

chapter has presented reasonable checks that should accompany the proper use of each gift. There should be a healthy fear about the potential abuse of prophecy, tongues, dreams and visions, and healing. Without biblical safeguards, we can find ourselves outside the mainstream of orthodoxy, swimming in a cultish, esoteric and antinomian religion. Many, in their enthusiasm, have fallen by the wayside in such a manner. We must "test everything; hold fast what is good" (1 Thess 5:21).

Having registered this caution, let us return to the process of overcoming our unwarranted fears. The biblical solution for this is love and faith. The apostle John tells us that "perfect love casts out fear" (1 Jn 4:18). Assurance of God's love and acceptance, and of his gifting of us for ministry should eject any fear. That love, when shared within a body which receives and encourages our gifts, causes us to grow confident in the use of our gifts as their benefit is perceived by all. The gifts of each of the authors of this book only matured in a congregational environment of love and forgiveness.

Fear is also overcome with faith (Ps 46:1-3; 112:7). As with any exchange of commodities, we give God our fears and apprehensions and take in their place a trust in God who is "our refuge and strength, a very present help in trouble." Sometimes it is helpful to imagine our fears all being packed in a bag which we give over to the Lord. In return, we can picture the strong arm of God reaching out of heaven, taking us by the hand, leading us through every threatening valley (Deut 33:27; Ps 31:5; 44:3).

Healing of Fears
Dealing concretely and practically with our fears is best accomplished by sharing the process with another person or a small group of people. In this context you can find support, encouragement, prayer and greater objectivity than

when alone. First, ask God to reveal any conscious or un-conscious fears you might have about the gifts mentioned in this book. Next, read each of the categories I have listed below. Discuss them if it seems appropriate. But restrain yourself from trying to exorcise fear by analyzing it. Define the area as it relates to you personally, and then pray that each of you would be delivered from the particular fear that is plaguing you. Last, covenant with one another to receive and exercise the gifts God gives to you. Inherent in this is the willingness to admit to your soul brother or sister re-curring bouts of fear.

The fears I am about to list are both intellectual and emo-tional. Some are superficial fears; others shake the very foundation of our personality. It is the latter which we seek to hide from others and never admit. Yet admission may be the first step to a life of liberation.

Loss of Job. If I begin to exercise some of these gifts I would lose my job. This honest admission was given by a friend over lunch. His theological community had written rules about the cessation of gifts, and to begin to practice them, something which he longed to do, put him in eco-nomic jeopardy.

Loss of Friends and Relatives. I fear I would lose friends and relatives who do not agree with me. Occasionally these gifts are a threat and an intrusion even to a peaceful marriage. Husbands and wives do not want to do anything to harm their marriage. Friends who before thought me merely *re-ligious,* may now think I am *fanatical.*

Controversy. If I should begin to manifest these gifts, I fear that too much controversy would be created. Some would make a fuss about what has happened, while others would ignore it and hope that it would quietly go away. That my gifts might somehow cause pain and division to an already fractured body makes me hesitate.

Being Unbiblical. I fear I might exercise these gifts unbiblically, practicing something which stems from my experience and not grounded in the Word of God. For years I have been taught that these gifts have ceased. To admit that they do exist is to repudiate the teaching I have received throughout my life.

Misleading Others. What if, by misusing these gifts, I mislead others, as well as hurting myself?

Loss of Control. If I should begin to manifest some of these gifts, I fear that I would lose control over the persona I have been projecting to the world. My image has been maintained by intellectual sophistication. To admit to an intuitive side of my life would mean a capitulation of my entire personality. I fear losing control and not being the director of the person I want to be.

Emotionalism. Through the exercise of these gifts I would become an emotional rag who could never pull myself together or be any dependable use to anyone. Like a broken dam, I would not be able to restrain the flood waters of emotion once they began to flow.

Loss of Objectivity. I fear that my intuition would always be playing tricks upon me. In such a state there would be no sound counsel for myself or anyone else.

Too Personal. If I opened myself to some of these gifts, I fear the Christian faith would become so personal that there would be no place for my real self to hide. Cerebral Christianity has always provided a buffer between what I believe and who I am. Such intimacy with the Holy Spirit and with others would remove that barrier.

Damaged Personality. These gifts would radically change my personality. I fear that God would have me down on the floor, rolling about and saying all kinds of embarrassing things to other people. That is a shock my personality could never endure.

In your small group, spend some time listing and praying through additional fears not mentioned here.

Who Do You Fear the Most?

For several days my grade-one son came home each night with wet, muddy jeans. As the chief washer, dryer and clothes folder in the family, I quickly tired of this additional, unnecessary work. Nose to nose, we had a frank conversation about dirty jeans. "But, Dad, Douglas pushes me in the mud every day after school," said Scott. Forgetting for the moment the Sermon on the Mount, I responded, "Well, what are you going to do about it?" No answer seemed forthcoming, so after pondering for a few minutes, I volunteered a solution. "Scott, are you afraid of Douglas?" "Yes," he said sheepishly. "Are you also afraid of the discipline of your father?" "Yes," he said enthusiastically. "Who do you fear the most, Douglas or me?" "You, Daddy!" "Then I don't want to see you come home again with dirty pants! Do you hear me?" "Yes, Daddy," he said. The message had clearly registered. From that day on we had no more problems with muddy pants after school.

I don't know what creative solution Scott brought to the problem, whether he pushed Douglas back or chose to avoid him after school. But it is clear that his greater fear of my discipline motivated him to overcome this minor fear.

There are many legitimate fears about manifesting controversial gifts. There are also many illegitimate fears. But the question remains: Who do we fear most? Is it not time that we feared God more than other people? Should we not fear more his judgment and displeasure over undeveloped gifts than what other would do or say if we begin to manifest these gifts? The answer to these questions is not hard, but the ability to do what is needed will require the wisdom of Solomon. God is not pleased when we use his gifts to destroy people and divide churches. But neither is he pleased with timidity over gifts which he has given to the church.

The great chapter on love, 1 Corinthians 13, is located

between two chapters on the use of gifts (1 Cor 12 and 14). Have you ever reflected on the significance of this? What it says to me is that only love will release us from fear and enable us to move through the relational traumas of restoring all the gifts to the church. Without love we will not know when to use these gifts or how to use them. Without love we will not be able to overlook the experimental mistakes of another believer or know how to lead them from fearfulness to faith. In love, we know that we prophesy only in part (1 Cor 13:9), not the whole, so we are careful of an arrogant spirit. Some day controversial gifts will no longer be needed (1 Cor 13:8), but love will always be the greatest need (1 Cor 13:13). So let us put off fear and put on love and exercise the gifts—all of them—with all the diligence and energy God provides.

Appendix
Gospel and Spirit:
A Joint Statement

As part of the development of *Theological Renewal* it is our intention to publish from time to time Occasional Papers, which will be sent to all subscribers, and cover subjects that are of special current interest and of theological significance for the charismatic renewal.

The series has an appropriate and auspicious beginning, with the *Joint Statement: Gospel and Spirit* prepared and agreed by the group of leaders, charismatic and non-charismatic, whose names appear below.

John Baker	Bruce Kay	Tom Smail
Colin Buchanan	Gordon Landreth	John Stott
John Collins	Robin Nixon	Tom Walker
Ian Cundy	Jim Packer	Raymond Turvey
Michael Harper	Harold Parks	David Watson
Raymond Johnston	Gavin Reid	

The statement explains itself but one cannot restrain a very joyful hallelujah that the so-called charismatic divide which caused so much misunderstanding and division in earlier years has now been not only bridged but to all intents and purposes closed, so that still varying insights can be shared in fully restored fellowship.

It was a great privilege for me, who am neither Anglican nor Evangelical (with a capital E, at any rate), to be allowed to share in the enriching fellowship that marked our discussions and the preparation of this Statement, and I pray this may be a foretaste of that unity in gospel and Spirit into which God is leading us all.   Thomas A. Smail

Background

A group nominated by the Church of England Evangelical Council and the Fountain Trust respectively met together for four valuable day conferences over a period of eighteen months. We are glad that we did so, and acknowledge that our failure to do so earlier may have helped to prolong unnecessary misunderstandings and polarisations.

We do not all see eye to eye on every point, but we thankfully recognise that what unites us is far greater than the matters on which some of us still disagree. We share the same evangelical faith, recognising each other as brothers in Christ and in the gospel, and we desire to remain in fellowship and to build yet stronger relationships of love and trust.

Our task has been to try to articulate widely held and representative attitudes among the so-called 'charismatic' and 'non-charismatic' leaders of Anglican Evangelicalism and to bring both to the bar of Holy Scripture. We have sought to understand each other's views better and to achieve closer harmony and correspondence through examining them all in the light of biblical teaching. We are now issuing this account of our progress, indicating both agreements and disagreements, in the hope that it may help to promote unity where there is discord, and mutual understanding where there has been mistrust.

We have been struck by the fact that in our discussions, differences of view (usually denoted by 'some' and 'others' [of us] in the text) have by no means always coincided with our 'charismatic' and 'non-charismatic' identifications.

The Charismatic Movement and Anglican Evangelicalism
The charismatic movement in the United Kingdom has evangelical roots, but is now both trans-denominational and trans-traditional, and embraces a very wide spectrum of views, attitudes and practices, not all originating from a recognised evangelical 'stable'. Anglican Evangelicalism also embraces a wide spectrum of views and emphases, as one would expect of a movement that has been developing and adapting itself over four centuries. In our exchanges we have tried to bear in mind the complexity of both constituencies and to avoid facile over-simplifications. Readers of this statement will judge how far we have succeeded.

We are united in thanking God for the real and obvious deeper acquaintance with Jesus Christ and his saving grace which charismatic renewal has brought to many individuals and the new life and vigour which many churches have come to enjoy as a result. We acknowledge however that with this there have been dangers and sometimes disasters, which have called for some self-criticism.

We rejoice too that renewal of spiritual life is manifestly not confined to 'charismatic' circles and churches, while we share a common sadness that much of the Church, both Evangelical and non-Evangelical, seems as yet to be untouched by true renewal in any form. In the quest for a quickening of the whole Church we believe ourselves substantially to be making common cause.

During the past thirty years sections of Anglican Evangelicalism have experienced a notable renewal of concern for the study and teaching of the doctrines of the faith. The main concern of the charismatic renewal, at least until recently, has been experimental rather than theological.

The resulting sense of polarisation and of being threatened at the level of one's priorities, purposes and pro-grammes may not have been justified, but has certainly been a potent cause of both tension and coolness. In our conversations we sought to overcome these inhibitions and build bridgeheads for future fellowship, trust and co-op-eration, and this we believe we have been enabled to do.

Christian Initiation and Baptism in the Spirit: Relating Terms and Experience

1. All gospel blessings given in Christ. We all agree that every spiritual blessing is given to us by God in and through our Lord Jesus Christ (Eph 1.3), so that every Christian is, in principle, complete, receiving fullness of life in him (Col 2.9-10). The Christ whom together we worship is the Jesus of the New Testament, God's Son incarnate who died for our sins, rose again and now lives and reigns. The gift of the Holy Spirit to believers is part of the ministry to them of our crucified, risen and ascended Lord, and the ministry of the Spirit is always to communicate, exalt and bear wit-ness to this glorified Christ.

We thus agree in our understanding of how the ministry of the Spirit is related to the Father and the Son, and in rejecting the idea that in the Spirit we receive something more wonderful than our Saviour, or something apart from him and the fullness of his saving grace.

2. Initiation into Christ. We are all convinced that accord-ing to the New Testament Christian initiation, symbolised and sealed by water-baptism, is a unitary work of God with many facets. This work is expressed by a cluster of partly overlapping concepts, including forgiveness, justification, adoption, regeneration, conversion (embracing repentance and faith in Jesus Christ as Lord and Saviour), new crea-tion, death, burial and resurrection in and with Christ, and the giving and reception of the Holy Spirit.

These concepts may be logically separated for consideration in teaching and learning; God's initiatory work is itself apprehended and experienced by different individuals in differing ways and time-scales; and certain aspects of it are in fact sometimes absent in evangelism, teaching, awareness and conscious experience. But essentially the concepts all belong together, since together they express the single full reality of the believer's incorporation into Christ, which leads to assurance of sonship, and power to live and serve in Christ. We are agreed on the need (i) to avoid trying to stereotype or straitjacket either the work of the Holy Spirit or the experience of individual Christians into a one, two or three-stage experience; (ii) to avoid presenting the work of the Spirit in separation from the work of the Son, since the Son gives the Spirit and the Spirit both witnesses to the Son and forms him in us; and (iii) to present the full range of Christ's salvation and gift for us in all our evangelism and teaching—ie to preach a complete, rather than a truncated, gospel.

3. Terminology: baptism in the Spirit. We are agreed that every Christian is indwelt by the Holy Spirit (Ro 8.9). It is impossible for anyone to acknowledge sin, confess Christ, experience new birth, enjoy the Saviour's fellowship, be assured of sonship, grow in holiness, or fulfil any true service or ministry without the Spirit. The Christian life is life in the Spirit. We all thank God for this gift.

In recent years there has been, as we said, a fresh enrichment in many Christians' Spirit-given experience of Christ, and in many cases they have called it 'baptism in the Holy Spirit'. Some of these people have seen their experience as similar to that of the disciples on the day of Pentecost, and other comparable events in Acts. Despite the observable parallels, however, there are problems attaching to the use of this term to describe an experience separated, often by a long period of time, from the person's initial conversion to Christ.

In the first place, this usage suggests that what is subnormal in the New Testament should be regarded as normal today: namely, that a long interval should elapse between new birth and any conscious realisation or reception of the Spirit's power.

In the second place, the New Testament use of the words 'baptise' and especially 'baptise into' stresses their initiatory content and context, and therefore refers to Christian initiation, rather than to a later enrichment of Christian experience.

However, we see that it may be hard to change a usage which has become very widespread, although we all agree in recognising its dangers. We would all emphasise that it must not be employed in a way which would question the reality of the work of the Spirit in regeneration and the real difference that this brings in experience from the outset. On that we are unanimous.

Some who speak of a post-conversion 'baptism in the Spirit' think of it mainly in terms of an empowering for service similar to the disciples' experience at Pentecost, though all are agreed that we should not isolate this side of the Spirit's work from his other ministries to and in the believer.

Some, stressing the experiential content of the term 'baptism in the Spirit', value it as having played a unique part in awakening Christians out of spiritual lethargy and bondage, and regard it as still having such a role in the future. Others, concentrating rather upon its initiatory implications, prefer to use it only to describe one aspect of new birth.

None of us wishes to deny the possibility or reality of subsequent experiences of the grace of God which have deep and transforming significance. We all affirm that a constant hunger and thirst after God should characterise every Christian, rather than any complacent claim to have 'arrived'. We urge one another and all our fellow-Christians to press on to know the Lord better, and thus to enter into the fullness of our inheritance in Christ (Ph 3.8-16).

4. Initial evidence of having received the gift of the Spirit. Although speaking in tongues is an initial phenomenon recorded on a number of occasions in connection with receiving the Holy Spirit in the book of Acts, the New Testament will not allow us to make it either the only, or the universal, or an indubitable evidence that this gift has been given. Indeed, we believe it is dangerous to appear to identify the Giver with the presence of any one of his gifts in isolation, however valuable that gift might be in itself. Nevertheless, it seems clear that the reception of the Spirit by Christians in the New Testament was something experienced, evidenced and often immediately perceived, rather than merely inferred (cf Ac 19.2, Ga 3.2).

When we ask what evidence of this reception we might expect, in the light of the New Testament records, the immediate answer must be a new awareness of the love, forgiveness and presence of God as our Father through Jesus Christ who is confessed as Lord, and the joyful spontaneous praise of God (whether in one's own tongue or another), issuing subsequently in a life of righteousness and obedience, and of loving service to God and man, a life which manifests gifts of the Spirit as well as spiritual understanding.

Evidence of H.S.'s presence

Spiritual Ethos

1. Emotion and intellect: doctrine and experience. We are aware that there is a real danger of exalting the intellect and understanding at the expense of the emotions. We know too that there is an equal danger of reacting against this into an anti-intellectual and emotionalist form of piety. We wish to assert, against both these extremes, the importance in faith and worship of the whole person.

We believe the mind must be involved in understanding the faith and applying it, and that the emotions, as well as the will, must be involved in our response to the truth and love of God, as well in his worship as in the compassionate service of our fellow men. Both doctrine and experience, word and Spirit, must go together, biblical doctrine testing, interpreting and controlling our experience, and experience fulfilling, incarnating and expressing our beliefs. Only so can we avoid the two extremes of a dead, rigid and barren orthodoxy, or an uncontrolled, unstable and fanatical emotionalism.

2. *Worship.* We believe that what are seen as characteristic features of 'evangelical' and 'charismatic' worship and spirituality will complement and enrich one another and correct the imbalances in each, although we recognise that in some situations the two so overlap already as to be almost indistinguishable. Many 'charismatic' gatherings would benefit from order, teaching, and some robustly doctrinal 'evangelical' hymns; just as many 'evangelical' services and prayer meetings would benefit from more spontaneity, greater participation, a more relaxed atmosphere, the gentle, loving wonder and praise of some renewal songs, and learning to listen to God in times of prayer and meditation.

3. *Faith: passive and active.* A different emphasis appears on occasion regarding the exercise of faith in the promises of the blessings offered to us by Christ in the gospel. 'Evangelicals' have sometimes laid all stress on the acceptance of Christ and his forgiveness and salvation at the outset, leading to commitment, and expected God then and thereafter to pour out his blessings in Christ without any necessary appropriating prayers of faith on our part—because it is his way to do more than we ask or think, and to give us many things without our asking. 'Charismatic' Christians, however, are among those who stress the need for the exercise

of expectant and appropriating faith in prayer for blessings and gifts God has promised to bestow upon us.

Both emphases can find support in the New Testament, and are complementary rather than mutually exclusive. Faith must both passively rest in the confidence of our Father's general goodness and generosity, trusting his wisdom to supply what we need as he sees it, but also on occasion pray actively and expectantly on the basis of his specific promises to his children and church, to claim their fulfilment as covenanted by him in answer to our prayers.

We all recognise further that sometimes our Father in his wisdom does not answer his children's prayers immediately, in order to teach us patiently and trustingly to wait upon him for his gifts. This saves us from lapsing from a living relationship into any automatic view of prayer, and helps us to trust him to give what we need and ask for in the way and at the time which he knows to be best for us.

Church Life, Structures and Relationships
1. The body of Christ. According to the New Testament the whole church is a charismatic community in which all are endowed with spiritual gifts *(charismata)* and are responsible for exercising them for the common good. The charismatic movement has been one of the forces which in recent years have begun healthily to correct an earlier excessive individualism, through recovery of the biblical emphasis upon the body of Christ.

We welcome this, with its corollary of every member being able to play a full part, through the Spirit's equipping, in the church's life, worship, witness and service. We recognise that under God this emphasis has prompted much hard work and patient ministry in the whole field of personal relationships and Christian life in community, and this we all applaud.

2. Structures. If these gains are to be assimilated, traditional ways of worship, ministry and congregational life must be modified and adapted. The doctrine and reality of the body of Christ cannot adequately be expressed through a pattern of ministry dependent chiefly, if not entirely, on one man, nor through exclusive use of a totally rigid 'set' pattern of worship.

Our Anglican heritage at both these points can and should be made flexible, so as to combine with, and contribute to, a genuinely corporate and Spirit-led church life. We see this as a necessary implication of the spiritual renewal of the church, and suspect that few yet realise either how important it is or how far it needs to go. Meanwhile, we welcome the preliminary experiments whereby both 'charismatic' and 'non-charismatic' Christians are currently seeking to discover for themselves what this principle might mean in practice.

3. Leadership and appointments. We believe a clergyman must see himself as an enabler and trainer of others to be the body of Christ in the place where they are. When the members of a church are renewed and revived so that they begin to exercise their gifts and to discover and develop their ministries, and lay leadership begins to grow, the pastor's work of oversight, teaching and leadership, and his function as a resource person, though changing perhaps in outward form, becomes more, not less, vital.

Accordingly, we believe that when the living becomes vacant in a charismatically-experienced church, great care must be taken that the functioning body of Christ in that place has a significant voice in the making of the next appointment. It also becomes important that a man be appointed who will gladly and skillfully lead a team, rather than expect to exercise a one-man pattern of ministry. This is just to say that the church, in making such an appointment, must keep up with what the Holy Spirit has been doing in that place, and not risk quenching him by ignoring, under-valuing or seeking to counter his work.

4. *Keeping churches and congregations together.* We have no new magical formula to hold churches together; there is only the old one of shared truth and mutual love, humility, tolerance and respect. Where churches split over these or any other matters, there are usually faults on both sides. Important guidelines will include: avoidance of any idea of first and second class Christians, which would engender pride, resentment and stubborn self-justification; willingness by those on all sides to respect each other's convictions, with openness to correction in the light of an honest reading of the New Testament; avoidance of quenching genuine spiritual gifts; respect for the authority of official leaders in the local church; and avoidance of splinter groups developing whose focus is something other (and therefore less) than Jesus Christ himself.

We also believe it important that those who disagree on these or other matters should be brought together in direct encounter face-to-face, rather than talking about each other without meeting to discuss their differences.

5. *Roman Catholics and renewal.* The renewing work of the Holy Spirit has led to Christians of different backgrounds having fellowship together in Christ and in the Spirit, as old prejudices and dividing barriers melt under the new power of God's love in their lives. Protestants and Roman Catholics often associate with each other in this way. We welcome this, but at the same time recognise these dangers:

a. A unity based on experience at the expense of doctrine would be less than the unity envisaged in the New Testament and would be dangerous in the long term.

b. Personal (and even corporate) renewal has not always meant the dropping of all anti-biblical or sub-biblical traditions and practices. We see the need to pray for and to encourage reformation by God's Word as well as renewal by his Spirit in all churches.

In the case of the Roman Catholic Church, however, a massive international community which has only recently begun to question its own historic stances, we recognise that God calls us to be realistic in our expectations, and to allow time (how long is not for us to say) for the forces of reformation and renewal to operate widely enough for changes in official formulations and interpretations of doctrine to become possible, where they are necessary.

Spiritual Gifts

1. Their nature, range and variety. A spiritual gift is a God-given capacity to serve others by his grace in a manner that edifies them in some way by the showing forth of Christ and his love. Spiritual gifts are listed in Romans 12, 1 Corinthians 12, Ephesians 4 and 1 Peter 4. We see no biblical warrant for isolating one set of gifts from other gifts listed elsewhere in the New Testament, nor for treating these lists as exhaustive.

Neither the context and terminology of 1 Corinthians 12 nor a comparison of the lists themselves will allow us to elevate one gift or set of gifts above another, although Paul indicates that in a meeting prophecy edifies the church, whereas tongues without interpretation do not. The comparative value of gifts depends upon the degree to which they edify, in the context in which they operate. Whilst observing that not all gifts and ministries have been equally in evidence throughout the Church's history, we declare our openness to receiving any spiritual gifts that are consonant with the New Testament, and see no reason why such gifts should not be given and exercised today. A few which have sometimes caused particular difficulties are singled out for special treatment later.

2. Praying for gifts. The Holy Spirit is sovereign in the distribution of gifts to particular individuals. The New Testament encourages the congregation to desire and to pray for spiritual gifts and to exercise those received for the good of others. A congregation may rightly pray expectantly for the Lord to supply a need, and where they see a gift or ministry required to meet that need, it is clearly appropriate to ask him for it.

3. Gifts for every member. The New Testament teaches that every Christian has already received some gift or gifts, and lays upon all the responsibility to recognise what is already given, and to manifest it. It also encourages all to desire, and therefore be open to receive and exercise, a spiritual gift and ministry of one sort or another, and sees the healthy functioning of a congregation as the body of Christ as dependent upon each one contributing in this way.

We believe this to be one of the most important truths highlighted by the charismatic movement, with far-reaching implications for the life and ministry of all our churches.

4. Their use, regulation and oversight. We believe it is vital that those who claim to have gifts should have those gifts tested by the leadership in the body of Christ in that place, and not be given *carte blanche* to exercise them as if above being questioned or corrected. Christians with recognised gifts should not be stifled, but rather encouraged in their ministry by the leadership. The exercise of gifts must be overseen by the eldership of the churches and by those more experienced in that field. Such gifts should be kept within the fellowship of the church, and not become a focal-point for a new 'gift-centred' fellowship.

On Particular Gifts and Ministries

1. Apostleship. Who, if any, of the first Christians shared the authority belonging to the Eleven and Paul, and on what grounds, may be debatable, but there is little doubt as to what that authority was. Through divine revelation and inspiration these men were authoritative spokesmen for, witnesses to, and interpreters of, God and his Son.

Their personal authority as teachers and guides—authority bestowed and guaranteed by the risen Christ—was final, and no appeal away from what they said was allowable. Such authority now belongs only to the scripture of the Old and New Testaments, under which all our churches and church leaders stand. Though latter-day ministries may in certain respects parallel apostolic functions, yet in their primary role as authoritative instructors the apostles have no successors, and any utterances or gestures of leadership today for which immediate inspiration is claimed must be evaluated by appeal to apostolic standards set forth in Holy Scripture. This is the Church's one sure safeguard against being spiritually tyrannised and misled, as has repeatedly happened in church history.

2. Prophecy. While estimates and interpretations of the New Testament phenomenon of prophecy vary, it is not identified there with the gift and ministry of teaching. Immediacy in receiving and declaring God's present message to men is the hallmark of New Testament prophecy, as of its Old Testament counterpart. Preaching may at times approximate more to prophecy, although its basic character is one of teaching and exhortation.

If the possibility of prophecy in the sense of speaking a word from the Lord under the direct prompting of the Holy Spirit is admissible today, what is said will be tested by its general agreement with scripture, and will not be accepted as adding materially to the Bible's basic revelation of God and his saving purposes in Christ. It will not be required that such utterances be cast in the first person singular, nor will those that are so cast be thought to have greater authority on that account.

3. Miracles. The living God is revealed to us in scripture as the Creator and Sustainer of all things, whose normal mode of operation is through the processes of nature and history, which he controls. We think there is need to unfold this truth more thoroughly at the present time, teaching Christians to discern the hand of God in all things. At the same time we all believe miracles can occur today. Despite the virtual impossibility of arriving at a satisfactory definition of 'miracles' in strictly scientific terms, we are in general agreement concerning their nature and purpose. We follow scripture in conceiving of miracles phenomenally, as occurrences of an unusual kind which bring awareness of the close presence of God, working out his will of salvation or judgment according to his word, and seeking by these manifestations to stir up the observers and beneficiaries (not to mention others) to new trust and worship. We believe that faith in the living God as delineated in scripture compels us to be open to the possibility of miracles in every age under the New Covenant, and that the Lord may call some Christians to particular ministries of a more obviously miraculous kind in particular times and places.

However we are never in a position to demand a miracle, since we may never dictate to our sovereign Lord how he shall work in answer to our prayers. Our business is to rest upon and claim his promises in obedience to his word, but to leave the means of the answer to his wisdom.

Over-concentration upon the miraculous can blind people to the manifold and wonderful everyday working of God in the world in 'non-miraculous' ways in the spheres of both creation and history. On the precise degree of expectation of miracles which is appropriate today we are not, however, completely agreed.

4. Healing. We believe that all true wholeness, health and healing come from God. We do not therefore regard 'divine healing' as being always miraculous. God's normal mode of healing is through the processes he has built into the human body and spirit. We also look forward to the resurrection, knowing that only then shall we be finally and fully freed from sickness, weakness, pain and mortality. At the same time we welcome the recovery by the Church of a concern for healing, and rejoice at those who have found new psychological or physical health through faith in Christ, and through Christian ministries and gifts of healing. But we also wish to express caution against giving wrong impressions and causing unnecessary distress through (i) making it appear that it is sinful for a Christian to be ill; (ii) laying too great a stress and responsibility upon the faith of the individual who is seeking healing; (iii) emphasising physical health more than the wholeness of the person; and (iv) setting non-medically-trained ministries and gifts of healing in opposition to the work and ministry of doctors and nurses.

5. *Exorcism.* Part of the ministry of Jesus Christ in the New Testament and in every age around the world is to set people free from the grip of satanic forces at work in or upon their personality. We are united in our belief in the existence of such personal spiritual powers, and in both the need and the possibility of Christ's deliverance. For he has been exalted far above all principalities and powers, and God has put them all under his feet. We all can testify that the regular ministry of word and sacrament, together with the prayer of faith which this evokes, can liberate people from bondage to the power of the devil. Sometimes, however, especially in clear cases of demon possession, exorcism may be necessary.

While not doubting that Christ gives to some people especially the necessary gifts to exercise this ministry safely and effectively in his name, it is an area fraught with dangers, which drive us to utter several cautionary warnings: (i) a preoccupation with demons (often to the neglect of the holy angels) is generally both dangerous and unbalanced, as is the tendency to attribute every unusual condition to demonic influence or presence; (ii) it is wise to avoid speaking of 'spirits' or 'demons' to those to whom we minister personally, unless this is absolutely unavoidable; (iii) the ministry of exorcism should not normally be exercised either by any Christian alone, or by any Christians without proper authority and oversight within the church; (iv) persons in need of this ministry will frequently need help at the psychological/emotional level of healing as well; (v) consultation with medical opinion (preferably sympathetic to a Christian viewpoint) is always highly desirable; (vi) careful pastoral follow-up is essential.

6. *Speaking in tongues.* Many Christians today testify to the value of this gift in their experience. Opinions vary as to how much of modern glossolalia corresponds with the New Testament phenomenon. Most of us would accept that some tongues-speaking, though not necessarily a heavenly language, is nevertheless divinely given and has spiritual and psychological value. We are also aware that a similar phenomenon can occur under occult/demonic influence, and that some such utterances may be merely psychological in origin and not necessarily edifying or beneficial at all.

Opinions also vary as to the value of this gift to the individual, and (with interpretation) to the church. We consider it necessary to hold to the balance of the New Testament in our general attitude to it, in accordance with 1 Corinthians 14, neither exalting it above all other gifts, nor despising it and forbidding its exercise (though always with interpretation if in public). But if we are true to the New Testament we shall seek to test it, as we do the other gifts in their public exercise, by its edifying effects; and we shall regulate its use scripturally, encouraging believers with this gift to 'pray with the understanding also' both in public and in private.

Conclusion: The Goal of Renewal

The goal of renewal is not merely renewed individuals but a renewed and revived Church, alive with the life of Christ, subject to the word of Christ, filled with the Spirit of Christ, fulfilling the ministry of Christ, constrained by the love of Christ, preaching the good news of Christ, and thrilled in its worship by the glory of Christ.

Such a Church alone can adequately portray Jesus Christ to the world. In preaching, writing and counselling, the Christ-centredness of the Christian life and the work of the Holy Spirit must constantly be emphasised, so that we may all together grow up fully into him, our glorious Head.

Notes

Chapter 1—Tidy Doctrine and Truncated Experience

[1]Thomas A. Smail, "Treasure and Trash and the Need to be Honest," *Renewal* 65 (October 1976):2.

[2]Bernard Ramm, *Protestant Biblical Interpretation* (Grand Rapids, Mich.: Baker Book House, 1970), pp. 98, 104.

[3]Merrill F. Unger, *New Testament Teaching on Tongues* (Grand Rapids, Mich.: Kregel Publications, 1971), p. 96.

[4]John F. Walvoord, *The Holy Spirit* (Wheaton, Ill.: Van Kampen Press, 1954), p. 179.

[5]Charles Caldwell Ryrie, *Dispensationalism Today* (Chicago: Moody Press, 1965).

[6]B. B. Warfield, *Counterfeit Miracles* (London: Banner of Truth Trust, 1972), pp. 3-31.

[7]Unger, *New Testament Teaching,* pp. 135-46.

[8]J. Grant Swank, Jr., "A Plea to Some Who Speak in Tongues," *Christianity Today* (February 28, 1975):12-13.

[9]"World Congress of Fundamentalists," *Christianity Today* (August 1975):422. See also John F. MacArthur, Jr., *The Charismatics* (Grand Rapids, Mich.: Zondervan, 1978), pp. 174-80; George Barton Cutter, *Speaking in Tongues: Historically and Psychologically Considered* (New Haven: Yale University Press, 1927).

[10]Walter Bauer, "τέλειος," *A Greek-English Lexicon of the New Testament,* ed. and trans. William F. Arndt and F. Wilbur Gingrich (Chicago:University of Chicago Press, 1957), p. 816.

[11]John R. W. Stott, *God's New Society* (Downers Grove, Ill.: InterVarsity Press, 1979), p. 107.

[12]Clark Pinnock, "An Evangelical Theology of the Charismatic Renewal," *Theological Renewal,* no. 7 (October-November 1977):31.

[13]MacArthur, *The Charismatics,* pp. 15-39.

[14]Harold Hunter, "Tongues Speech: A Patristic Analysis," *Journal of the Evangelical Theological Society* (June 1980), p. 136.

[15]Michael Green, *Evangelism in the Early Church* (Grand Rapids, Mich.: Eerdmans, 1970), p. 201.

[16]"The Letter of the Churches of Vienna and Lugdunum to the Churches of Asia and Phrygia," in *Ante-Nicene Fathers,* ed. Alexander Roberts and James Donaldson, 10 vols. (Grand Rapids, Mich.: Eerdmans, 1956), 8:782.

[17]Eusebius *Church History* 3. 39. 9.

[18]Quoted in James W. Jones, *Filled with New Wine* (New York: Harper & Row, 1974), p. 56.

[19]Eusebius *Church History* 5. 7. 1-6 and Irenaeus *Against Heresies* 2. 32. 4.

[20]Hippolytus *Apostolic Tradition* 1. 15.

[21]Tertullian *A Treatise on the Soul* 9.

[22]Tertullian *Against Marcion* 5. 8.

[23]Cyril of Jerusalem *Catechetical Lectures* 16.12 and 17.37, as noted in Michael Green, *I Believe in the Holy Spirit* (Grand Rapids, Mich.: Eerdmans, 1975), p. 172.

[24]Origen *Against Celsus* 1. 46 and *De Principiis* 1. 3. 7-8 and 2. 7. 2

[25]Augustine *Retractions* 1. 13. 7, quoted in Paul Elbert, "Calvin and Spiritual Gifts," *Journal of the Evangelical Theological Society* 22, no. 3 (September 1979):253.

[26]Martien Parmentier, "Two Early Charismatic Movements: Montanism and Messalianism," *Theological Renewal,* no. 3 (June-July 1976):17.

[27]James G. S. S. Thomson, "Spiritual Gifts," *Baker's Dictionary of Theology,* ed. Everett F. Harrison, (Grand Rapids, Mich.: Baker Book House, 1960), p. 500.

[28]*The Journal of John Wesley* 3.490, quoted in A. Skevington Wood, "John Wesley, Theologian of the Spirit," *Theological Renewal,* no. 6 (June-July 1977):31.

[29]Elbert, "Calvin and Spiritual Gifts," p. 251.

[30]Quoted in Michael Harper, *As at the Beginning* (London: Hodder & Stoughton, 1965), pp. 19-20.

Chapter 2—Thus Says the Lord: Prophecy and Discernment

[1]Carl E. Armerding, "Prophecy in the Old Testament," *Handbook of Biblical Prophecy,* ed. Carl E. Armerding and W. Ward Gasque (Grand Rapids, Mich.: Baker Book House, 1977), p. 62.

[2]J. A. Motyer, "Prophecy, Prophets," *New Bible Dictionary,* ed. J. D. Douglas (Grand Rapids, Mich.: Eerdmans, 1962), p. 1039.

[3]Gerhard Friedrich, "προφήτης," *Theological Dictionary of the New Testament,* ed. Gerhard Kittel and Gerhard Friedrich, trans. Geoffrey W. Bromiley, 10 vols. (Grand Rapids, Mich.: Eerdmans, 1964-76), 6:849

[4]Simon Tugwell, *Did You Receive the Spirit?* (London: Darton, Longman and Todd, 1972), p. 60.

[5]Bauer, "ζηλόω," *Greek-English Lexicon,* p. 338.
[6]*Theological Renewal Occasional Paper,* no. 1 (April-May 1977):10. The entire statement is reprinted in the appendix.
[7]Motyer, "Prophecy, Prophets," p. 1045.
[8]John F. Walvoord, *The Holy Spirit at Work Today* (Chicago: Moody Press, 1973), pp. 13-14.
[9]*Theological Renewal Occasional Paper,* no. 1 (April-May 1977):10.
[10]James D. G. Dunn, "According to the Spirit of Jesus," *Theological Renewal,* no. 5 (February-March 1977):18.
[11]Bruce Yocum, *Prophecy* (Ann Arbor: Word of Life, 1976), p. 63.
[12]As quoted in Richard J. Foster, *Celebration of Discipline* (San Francisco: Harper & Row, 1978), p. 110.
[13]Donald Bridge and David Phypers, *Spiritual Gifts and the Church* (Downers Grove, Ill.: InterVarsity Press, 1973), pp. 66-67.
[14]Dunn, "According to the Spirit of Jesus," p. 17.
[15]Yocum, *Prophecy,* pp. 103-21.
[16]Arthur Wallis, *God's Chosen Fast* (London: Victory Press, 1968).

Chapter 3—Dreams and Visions: God's Picture Language
[1]Ambrose *Letter* 51. 14.
[2]John A. Sanford, *Dreams: God's Forgotten Language* (New York: Lippincott, 1968).
[3]Gerhard von Rad, *Old Testament Theology,* 2 vols. (London: Oliver and Boyd, 1965), 2:59.
[4]Alan Richardson, ed., *A Theological Word Book of the Bible* (New York: Macmillan, 1950).
[5]Ibid., p. 277.
[6]Merrill F. Unger, "Dream," *Baker's Dictionary of Theology,* p. 173.
[7]"Letter of the Smyrnaeans on the Martyrdom of Saint Polycarp," in *The Apostolic Fathers,* ed. J. B. Lightfoot (Grand Rapids, Mich.: Eerdmans, 1976), p. 110.
[8]Irenaeus *Against Heresies* 4. 20. 8-12.
[9]Origen *Against Celsus* 1. 46, 48 and 66.
[10]Tertullian *A Treatise on the Soul* 47; see also 43-49. Cf. preface to *The Passion of the Holy Martyrs Perpetua and Felicitas.*
[11]Cyprian *Epistles* 53.5 and 33. 1.
[12]Augustine *Letters* 158 and 159. Throughout his writings, Augustine gives many examples of dreams and visions. One of the best known is the dream of his mother, Monica, in which she saw her son standing with her in faith. This dream helped her to persevere in her prayers for his conversion (Augustine *Confessions* 3. 11. 19).

[13]Jerome *Letter* 22. 30.

[14]Morton Kelsey, *God, Dreams and Revelations* (Minneapolis: Augsburg 1974).

[15]James Ash, Jr., "The Decline of Prophecy in the Early Church," *Theological Studies* (June 1976):227-51.

[16]See Kelsey, *God, Dreams and Revelations,* p. 155.

[17]Ibid., p. 174.

[18]As quoted by Kelsey, *God, Dreams and Revelations,* p. 177. The views of Aquinas profoundly influenced the thinking of the Western Church for at least seven hundred years. Even the Reformers did not escape the Aristotelian influence entirely. Descartes, the seventeenth-century French philosopher, further popularized Aristotelian thinking. Following him, few Western theologians of name dared risk their standing by paying respect to "supernatural" phenomena.

[19]Reports of various charismatic manifestations have come from such movements as the Huguenots, Jansenists, the Quakers (especially in the seventeenth century), the Wesleyan revival in England and the Great Awakening in America.

[20]Alan Heinurt and Perry Miller, eds., *The Great Awakening,* The American Heritage Series (New York: Bobbs-Merrill, 1967), pp. 147-51.

[21]Kelsey, *God, Dreams and Revelations,* pp. 184-86.

[22]Raymond Edman, *Finney Lives On* (Minneapolis: Bethany, 1971), pp. 30-37.

[23]Michael Harper, *As at the Beginning,* pp. 51-53.

[24]David Wilkerson, *The Vision* (New York: Pyramid Books, 1974). Demos Shakarian, *The Happiest People on Earth* (Waco, Texas: Word, 1975). Harold Bredesen, *Yes, Lord* (Plainfield, N. J.: Logos, 1972).

[25]David M. Howard, *By the Power of the Spirit* (Downers Grove, Ill.: Inter-Varsity Press, 1973), pp. 65-68.

[26]Morton Kelsey, *Dreams–A Way to Listen to God* (New York: Paulist Press, 1978), p. 55.

[27]Harold Bredesen, *Yes, Lord,* pp. 161-64.

[28]John and Paula Sandford, *The Elijah Task* (Plainfield, N. J.: Logos, 1977), p. 174.

[29]Ibid., pp. 174-81.

[30]John A. Sanford, *Dreams: God's Forgotten Language,* p. 118.

Chapter 4—Tongues: The Biggest Christian Friendship and Oneness Buster of the Century

[1]The title for this chapter is borrowed from Peter E. Gillquist, *Let's Quit Fighting about the Holy Spirit* (Grand Rapids, Mich.: Zondervan, 1974),

p. 87.

[2]Johannes Behm, "γλῶσσα, ἐτερόγλωσσος," *Theological Dictionary of the New Testament,* 1:725-26.

[3]John Kildahl, *The Psychology of Speaking in Tongues* (New York: Harper & Row, 1972), p. 74, quoted in the argument of MacArthur, *The Charismatics,* p. 177.

[4]Charles E. Hummel, *Fire in the Fireplace* (Downers Grove, Ill.: Inter-Varsity Press, 1978), pp. 198-99.

[5]Larry Christenson, *Speaking in Tongues* (Minneapolis: Dimension Books, 1968), p. 20. Christenson suggests that those who *heard* the tongues of Pentecost were living in Jerusalem and hence there was no language barrier with those who *spoke* in tongues. I must disagree. The point of Acts is that these were pilgrims to the city from all over the world, come to celebrate the feast, and that the language barrier was overcome by this gift to Jesus' disciples.

[6]See, for example, Howard, *By the Power of the Holy Spirit,* p. 117. Also see Tugwell, *Did You Receive the Spirit?* pp. 73-74; Ronald A. N. Kydd, "Glossolalia and God," *Crux* 9, no. 3 (May 1972):18-23.

[7]George E. Gardiner, *The Corinthian Catastrophe* (Grand Rapids, Mich.: Kregel Publications, 1974), p. 43.

[8]MacArthur, *The Charismatics,* pp. 174-75.

[9]Oswald Sanders, *The Holy Spirit and His Gifts* (Grand Rapids, Mich.: Zondervan, 1970), p. 125.

[10]W. G. Putman, "Tongues, Gift of," *New Bible Dictionary,* pp. 1286-87.

[11]William J. Samarin, "Sacred and Profane," *Crux* 9, no. 3 (May 1972):4. See also William J. Samarin, *Tongues of Men and Angels* (New York: Macmillan, 1972).

[12]Ibid., pp. 4-11.

[13]C. H. Dodd, *The Epistle of Paul to the Romans* (London: Hodder and Stoughton, 1932), p. 135.

[14]Thomson, "Spiritual Gifts," *Baker's Dictionary of Theology,* p. 500.

[15]Ibid., p. 22.

[16]Arnold Bittlinger, *Gifts and Graces* (Grand Rapids, Mich.: Eerdmans, 1967), p. 51.

[17]"The Christianity Today Gallup Poll: An Overview," *Christianity Today* (Dec. 21, 1979), p. 14.

[18]Jamie Buckingham, *Kathryn Kuhlman: Daughter of Destiny* (Plainfield, N. J.: Logos, 1976), p. 45.

[19]Behm, *Theological Dictionary of the New Testament,* 1:722.

[20]Thomas A. Smail, *Reflected Glory* (London: Hodder and Stoughton, 1975), p. 43.

[21]Tugwell, *Did You Receive the Spirit?* p. 70.

Chapter 5—The Recovery of Healing Gifts
[1]Karl Barth, *Church Dogmatics*, III/4 (Edinburgh: T. & T. Clark, 1961), p. 369.
[2]D. C. Westermann, "Salvation and Healing in the Community: The Old Testament Understanding," *International Review of Mission* (January 1972), p. 10.
[3]Charles Farah, *From the Pinnacle of the Temple* (Plainfield, N. J.: Logos, 1979), pp. 71-72.
[4]Franz Delitzsch, *Biblical Commentary on the Prophecies of Isaiah*, 2 vols. (Grand Rapids, Mich.: Eerdmans, 1969), 2:316.
[5]Morton Kelsey, *Healing and Christianity* (New York: Harper & Row, 1973), p. 54.
[6]Ibid., p. 59.
[7]As quoted in Kelsey, *Healing and Christianity*, p. 185.
[8]Evelyn Frost, *Christian Healing: A Consideration of the Place of Spiritual Healing in the Church of Today in the Light of the Doctrine and Practice of the Ante-Nicene Church* (London: A. R. Mowbray and Co. Ltd., 1940), p. 68.
[9]Willem Jan Kooiman, *By Faith Alone: The Life of Martin Luther* (London: Lutterworth Press, 1954), p. 192.
[10]Clark Pinnock, "Opening the Church to the Charismatic Dimension," *Christianity Today* 25, no. 11 (June 12, 1981):16.
[11]Foster, *Celebration of Discipline*, p. 54.
[12]Kelsey, *Healing and Christianity*, p. 8.

Chapter 6—Equipping for Spiritual Gifts
[1]Oswald Chambers, *My Utmost for His Highest* (Toronto: McLelland and Stewart, 1953), p. 291.
[2]Douglas Hyde, *Dedication and Leadership* (Notre Dame University Press, 1966), p. 35, emphasis added.
[3]Ibid., p. 42, emphasis added.
[4]Howard A. Snyder, *The Problem of Wineskins* (Downers Grove, Ill.: InterVarsity Press, 1976), p. 99.
[5]Peter Gillquist, *The Physical Side of Being Spiritual* (Grand Rapids, Mich.: Zondervan, 1979), p. 126.
[6]George Mallone, *Furnace of Renewal* (Downers Grove, Ill.: InterVarsity Press, 1981), pp. 43-76.
[7]Lawrence O. Richards, *A Theology of Church Leadership* (Grand Rapids, Mich.: Zondervan, 1980).